THE ECONOMICS OF
COLLECTIVE BARGAINING

The Economics of Collective Bargaining

By P. FORD

Emeritus Professor of Economics
University of Southampton

SECOND EDITION REVISED

BASIL BLACKWELL
OXFORD
1964

First printed in 1958
Revised 1964

Printed in Great Britain for BASIL BLACKWELL & MOTT, LTD.
by A. R. MOWBRAY & CO. LIMITED in the City of Oxford
and bound at the KEMP HALL BINDERY

PUBLICATIONS BY THE DEPARTMENT OF ECONOMICS, THE UNIVERSITY, SOUTHAMPTON:

The Southampton Survey (undertaken at the request of the Southampton County Borough Council), by Professor P. Ford, B.Sc.(Econ.), Ph.D., and Mr. C. J. Thomas, B.Sc., M.Sc.(Econ.).

   1. Industrial Prospects of the Southampton Region.
   2. Shops and Planning.
   3. Housing Targets.
   4. Problem Families (with E. T. Ashton, M.A.).

Parliamentary Papers Series, by Professor P. and Mrs. G. Ford.

   1. Hansard's Catalogue and Breviate of Parliamentary Papers, 1696–1834.
   2. Select List of British Parliamentary Papers, 1833–1899.
   3. A Breviate of Parliamentary Papers, 1900–1916.
   4. A Breviate of Parliamentary Papers, 1917–1939.
   5. A Guide to Parliamentary Papers.
   6. A Breviate of Parliamentary Papers, 1940–1954.
   7. Luke Graves Hansard's Diary, 1814–1841.

Coastwise Shipping and the Small Ports, by Professor P. Ford and Mr. J. A. Bound, B.Sc.(Econ.).

PREFACE TO THE FIRST EDITION

THE purpose of this book is to assist students of economics, whether in the university, in workers' classes or in business, to look at the realities of the labour market in the light of current economic theory. It has been built from actual cases drawn from Parliamentary and official inquiries, wage awards, trade union reports, etc. As it is important that these matters should be discussed in the work-a-day world of business and trade union activity without the undue use of technical terms, which can often be dispensed with when the distinctions implied have become part of one's way of thinking, the argument has been set out in non-technical language.

I hope that students from the trade union movement with whom I have had the pleasure of discussing these matters over many years will feel that I have tried to answer their questions and that the work has profited by the interchange of ideas and experience.

The book is concerned with collective bargaining as such, and though it discusses some of the problems of union policy to which this gives rise in conditions of full employment, it does not deal with Government wage policy, which involves monetary and political questions of quite a different order requiring separate and extended treatment.

I am much indebted to Miss D. Marshallsay, B.A., A.L.A., for preparing the index and for her great care in checking the references. My thanks are also due to Professor Armstrong for reading the typescript and giving me the benefit of his comments, and to Mrs. P. Dunn for typing the book.

PREFACE TO THE SECOND EDITION

THE new edition of this book brings within its scope the important disputes, wage inquiries and agreements, the phases of 'wage restraint', the repercussions on union policy of the National Incomes Commission and National Economic Development Council, and the attitude of T.U.C., up to the Brighton Congress 1963. The book is concerned with collective bargaining as such, and, as indicated in the Preface to the first edition, does not move out of this field to deal with the larger aspects of Government wages policy involving monetary and political considerations.

The intention of the book remains to invite students of economics to walk round the labour market, bringing their theory with them, since it helps one to see things the significance of which might otherwise be missed.

CONTENTS

The Economics of Collective Bargaining

INTRODUCTION

A STUDY of the economics of collective bargaining between trade unions and employers has a double interest. At a time when the wages of 90 per cent of the employed population are regulated either by collective agreements negotiated between unions and employers, or by wages councils representing both sides and established by the State for the express purpose of enabling unorganized and poorly organized workers to enjoy some of the advantages of those in trade unions, its practical interest needs no emphasis. But to an economist it has an attractive theoretical interest as well. A recognized part of his technique is that of constructing simplified working models of the dominant factors in some problem and investigating their behaviour; with these first results in hand he can approach the problem again to see what they would be when account is taken of all the complications introduced by special circumstances, by the law, and the working of economic institutions of various kinds. Sometimes, as with simple price problems, these first results stand, and there is little more to be said. But in an investigation of the influence of trade unions on wages this is not the case, for their policies are affected by the way they are organized, the extent of the differences in occupation and outlook amongst the members and the internal pressures these generate, and by the powers and position of the leaders. The economist is thus at once taken to the behaviour of the rank and file of ordinary men and women members who pay their subscriptions, vote or fail to vote in union ballots and the kinds of matters about which they will or will not go on strike. It is the task of disentangling the effects of theoretical principles from those traceable to the institutions and behaviour of the work-a-day world which is intriguing. This need not throw any chill on the warm sympathy with which the economist of the late nineteenth and of the twentieth century, in contrast to his predecessors a hundred years earlier, approached the study of trade unionism. And the loud denunciations by extremists of 'capitalist exploiters' and 'labour monopolists' may encourage him to enjoy a slightly mischievous inquisitiveness about what is actually going on behind the shouting on the front of the stage.

1

To anyone interested in economic theory, the problem to be solved is how far the wage structure differs from what it would have been in the absence of trade unions; and if it does, what are the economic processes by which the difference has been brought about. Put in this way, the question certainly takes us to the heart of the matter, but immediately reveals its difficulty. How are we to discover what wages would have been in the different trades in the absence of unions? We do not get much light on it by comparing wages in organized industries with those in industries neither organized into unions nor regulated by wages councils, for only 10 per cent of the working population are in that condition. Before 1939, perhaps the largest group of unorganized workers were women engaged in domestic work and retail distribution. But since a large proportion of them now have their wage rates determined by the Catering Wages Commission or by wages councils or by bodies dealing with institutional domestic staff, there are now left only those in the contracting field of private domestic work whose pay is the result of a process of individual bargains between workers and mistresses: and even there the rate is obviously largely influenced by wages fixed in institutions and the catering trades. We should be helped a great deal by detailed studies of the history of wages in various trades in relation to the development of the respective trade unions and their policies. One hundred per cent trade unions do not suddenly appear in hitherto entirely unorganized industries— in which case we could study 'before' and 'after'—but take time to grow into a position of bargaining strength: and one would have, at the same time, to look at adjacent industries using the same kind of labour. We are better provided with studies of this kind than our predecessors were, e.g. those by Phelps Brown, but there is still much to be done. The eight great reports on Earnings and Hours in various industries issued by the Board of Trade, 1900–1913, have been used by economic historians interested in the progress of the standard of life, but seem not to have been yet fully worked over by economists with their problems of theory in mind.

A wage may be negotiated by a union, yet the union may not have 'obtained' it, or all of it. A rising demand for labour in an expanding industry might of its own account lead to a rise of pay, whether there is a trade union or not; what has to be explained is any excess of wages over and above this figure which has been obtained by the collective bargaining process itself. This may be a larger or smaller part of the negotiated increase. The list of agreed wage increases published periodically in the *Ministry of Labour Gazette* represents the outside margin which includes that part due to collective bargaining in the precise sense we have given it. In conditions of full employment, whether as defined by Patrick Colquhoun in 1815 as 'that great blessing in which the demand for labour is somewhat more than the supply',[1] or by Beveridge as the state in which there are more vacant jobs than unemployed men, a seller's rather than a buyer's market for labour, wages can be expected to rise whether there are active unions or not. This was noted in separate industries long ago. Thus, Mr. Robinson in evidence before the Commissioners on Trade Unions, 1867, stated that he did not think unions had raised wages to a higher point than they would have reached without a union, and gave examples of trades where there had been little advance although there was a strong union and of other trades where wages had risen although there was no union.[2] Other evidence of the same character is quoted by T. Brassey in *Work and Wages*, 1872. Drawing upon the experience of his father's great firm in overseas railway building, he points out that 'our operatives have but a faint conception of the rise of wages which has taken place abroad where Trades Unions do not exist'.[3] B. C. Roberts, over eighty years later, points out that whereas in 1952 weekly money wage rates of engineers with a militant union had risen from 100 in 1938 to 209, and those of coalminers, also with a militant union, had risen to 369, those of agricultural workers, where unionism was relatively weak, had risen to 319.[4] And, especially in a period of inflation, the basis of many claims for wages increases has been that prices, output and profits in the industry concerned have all risen, and that 'the industry can afford to pay them'.

At this point one could declare that it is impossible to disentangle the effects of trade unions' collective bargaining from those of the economic circumstances of industry and that not only is it useless to pursue this will-o'-the-wisp, but that it is not even worth pursuing.

[1] P. Colquhoun. *Wealth, Power and Resources of the British Empire.* 2nd ed. 1815. p. 426.

[2] *Organization and Rules of Trade Unions and other Associations.* R. Com. 10th Rep., mins. of ev. q. 18,988 and p. 57; 1867–68 [3980–VI] xxxix.

[3] T. Brassey. *Work and Wages.* 1872. pp. 43–7.

[4] B. C. Roberts. *Trade Union Behaviour.* In, J. T. Dunlop (ed.). *The Theory of Wage Determination.* 1957. p. 120.

For trade unions have to be regarded as a permanent part of our economic machinery, and the thing that matters in the practical working of the economy, both in their effects on costs and on the relative attractiveness of different industries, are the wages actually negotiated: how much of these represent excess over the wages which would have been established in the absence of a union is of no importance. Both conclusions are, at any rate to begin with, unacceptable, since there may be a way out of the difficulty through an appeal to theory. It may be possible to construct simplified theoretical models of the major forces at work which bear so close a resemblance to many of the different cases on the labour market in which trade unions and employers are involved, that they can give us an approximate idea of the part this particular component may play in determining wage rates. But it is the second part of the problem which is of most interest to the trade unionist, the employer and the consumer of the product: if trade unions can raise wages above the level they would settle at if there were no unions, where does the increase come from? This is the form in which the problem presents itself in practical life, and it is one to which theory must give an answer.

THE COLLECTIVE AGREEMENT AND THE BARGAINING PROCESS

The Standard Rate and the Collective Agreement

FUNDAMENTAL to British trade unionism are the standard rate of wages and its regulation by collective agreement. Through the spread of wage agreements both are now widely understood, but there are certain features of their form and substance, and the processes by which they are negotiated which need to be kept in mind in working out the economic theory relating to them.

The standard rate is intended to apply to all workers of the same class doing the same work in the same conditions. Whether the firms which employ them are large or small, well managed or ill managed, prosperous or shaky is irrelevant: the worker's wage should not depend on differences of organization or success outside his control. The rate so fixed is a minimum, not a maximum, and sometimes, especially in conditions of full employment, firms pay more than the standard rate in order to recruit and keep a specially competent staff. It is the rate which is standard, not earnings, for in some industries it takes the form of a list of piece rates, which will yield the individual operatives greater or smaller earnings according to their output.

Implied in the standard rate is the performance of a certain amount of work, which may be roughly understood on both sides and expressed by the agreed hours of work, or may be measured by the number of meters to be read, the stretch of roadside verge to be cleared, the amount of ploughing to be done, the number of machines to be looked after, the number of men required in a gang to perform particular operations. It may be protected by understandings on what rates should be paid and what grades of men should be used if new machinery is introduced. Alterations of working conditions may be held to alter the amount, strain or unpleasantness of work, so that extra payments may be required

5

on account of them, e.g. 'dirty money' for handling difficult or unpleasant cargoes.

The American term for a collective agreement, 'labour contract', implies a document setting forth in precise detail what the conditions are. English collective agreements, on the other hand, vary from simple, short statements setting out the rate, overtime rates, the length of the working day, etc., to more elaborate instruments governing the whole conditions of employment, from wages to hours, numbers of apprentices, changes of machinery, holidays and the procedure for settling small disputes and preventing local grievances from developing into wider disputes by workshop and shipyard discussions, by 'neutral' committees drawn from associated works, local conferences and meetings between unions and employers at a 'national' level. In Britain collective bargaining thus takes place within a framework of understandings and conventions.

Some of the arrangements made in these agreements are of great interest from an economic point of view. Most unions aim at a 'national agreement' covering the wages of their members throughout the country. Such a national agreement may provide for a uniform national wage, since the union may insist that a craftsman is a craftsman wherever he happens to be. But it may mean simply a national agreement on district rates. If the industry is prosperous in one area but lagging in another, district rates may be accepted to protect both; and as water undertakings, bakeries and laundries in Newcastle do not compete with those in Kent or South Wales, separate district rates may give the best results, since the low wage area cannot 'drag down' the high wage area. Though the different coal-producing districts had some different as well as some common markets, it was this fear of the low wage district undercutting the high wage district which lay behind the miners' long struggle in the inter-war years for a national minimum wage and a national agreement, an aim not achieved until June 1942 and March 1943.

The Conditions of Successful Collective Bargaining

Events which occurred during the outbreaks of large-scale industrial conflict in 1911–13 led to an attempt to formulate some of the conditions of successful collective bargaining. In a railway dispute the companies had refused to meet a deputation of their men, accompanied by their Secretary, Mr. R. Bell, who was not, of course, in the employment of the company, and a ballot vote showed an overwhelming majority in favour of a strike for their 'Programme' and the principle of recognition of the union. A Royal Commission on the working of their conciliation agreement had felt it necessary to say that the companies could not be expected to permit intervention between themselves and the men on questions of discipline and management.[1] In a dispute affecting dockers in London and the Medway, also, the employers had refused to meet the men's representatives.[2] Furthermore, there had been strikes in Northumberland in connection with the Eight Hours' Agreement signed by the men's representatives, in the London taxicab trade in 1913 because circumstances meant that some clauses of an agreement would have had the effect of reducing the men's wages, as well as of London carters. Non-recognition, repudiated agreements and the attitude of employers not parties to an agreement were thus critical matters. In 1912 an Industrial Council composed of representatives of both employers and trade unionists was asked to inquire into the best method of securing the due fulfilment of industrial agreements and how far and in what manner they should be enforced.[3] The report argued that industrial agreements could not be compared with commercial contracts because of the peculiar conditions attaching to them, some of which were the numbers of persons involved, the difficulty of ascertaining beforehand the exact wishes of those represented, and the circumstances surrounding trade movements which made it difficult to obtain a well-defined authority able to enter into a settlement. Amongst its positive conclusions were that the fulfilment of agreements was easiest and most successful in those industries where there was the greatest amount of organization both of employers and workers, and that parties to an agreement should be able to apply to the Board of Trade for an inquiry whether the terms of an agreement covering a trade or district should be made obligatory on persons not members of associations represented by the signatories. Both flexibility in and means of settling differences of interpretation were required. The Council stressed that the success of collective agreements had

[1] *Railway Conciliation and Arbitration Scheme of 1907.* R. Com. Rep.; 1911 Cd. 5922, xxix. P. and G. Ford. *Breviate of Parliamentary Papers, 1900–1916.* 1957. p. 202.

[2] *Present Disputes Affecting Transport Workers in the Port of London and on the Medway.* Rep.; 1912–13 Cd. 6229, xlvii. *Breviate, 1900–1916.* p. 203.

[3] *Industrial Agreements.* Industrial Council. Rep.; 1913 Cd. 6952, xxviii. *Breviate, 1900–1916.* p. 205.

B

been due mainly to the recognition on both sides of the moral obligations involved. How far do the present machinery and processes of negotiation meet the difficulties?

1. THE BARGAINING UNIT

Both the terms which unions aim at putting into agreements, the processes by which they are negotiated and the means by which they are enforced are influenced by the way in which unions are organized, the groups of workers they include and therefore the pressures within them. British trade unions have been built up experimentally over a century and a half, and show a great variety of type. Some, such as the Transport and General Workers' Union, are great unions, embracing all types of workers, skilled and unskilled, men and women. Others restrict their membership to skilled men of the same craft, closely bound together by common interests. The membership of some, such as the cotton textile unions or the London Society of Compositors, is concentrated mainly in a limited region, of others in a limited number of regions, as in the case of the National Union of Mineworkers, while that of others may be scattered all over the country, like that of the National Union of Agricultural Workers. The members may be in the employment of large numbers of small firms, such as those of the Distributive and Allied Workers; or be composed of groups of men of varying degrees of skill, some concentrated in great rail centres, others living in the countryside, but all working for one employer, as in the case of the National Union of Railwaymen. This apparently untidy pattern is in sharp contrast to the neat list of forty-seven clearly defined industrial groups into which the German unions were organized as part of a single plan.[1] Organized at different dates and in varying climates of social ideals, the unions' constitutions contain an endless variety of experiments in organizing constituencies, methods of voting, the use of the referendum, the position and control of officers, the degree of centralization, the persons to whom power is given to call strikes or to terminate them, etc. Too long neglected by students of democratic institutions, these constitutional arrangements have now been

[1] W. S. Sanders. *Trade Unionism in Germany*. Fabian Society, 1916. pp. 14, 15.

skilfully analysed by V. L. Allen.[1] Most of these constitutions and procedures we can take for granted, since we are concerned only in so far as they affect the union's economic policy, the manner in which it is negotiated and put into force, and its strength as a bargaining unit.

Trades Union Congress has been led to discuss and to promote what it considers to be the most effective bargaining organization. The first type to prove itself as a bargaining unit was, of course, the craft union. 'The creation of a trade union is possible only when an identity of interests exists between groups of workers. This is the basis of all combinations, and the more related the interests of given groups of workers, the more likelihood there is that combination will be constant and durable.'[2] Though criticized by contemporary socialists for exclusiveness, their capacity to pay relatively high subscriptions and to employ full-time officers, etc., made them the pioneers in the nineteenth century of stable unions able to make enduring collective bargains. With the rise of unions of semi-skilled and unskilled workers based on varied principles of organization and the enthusiastic conquest of unoccupied territory which went on apace at the end of the nineteenth and the first two decades of the present century, unions soon began to 'meet' and 'overlap' and boundary disputes became a frequent consequence. Its endeavour to settle boundaries and to prevent 'poaching' naturally led T.U.C. to consider what was the most effective bargaining unit. Hull Congress, 1924, declared that the number of unions should be reduced to a minimum, that unions should be organized by industry and linked up to secure a united front. In an able memorandum presented to the Scarborough Congress, 1925, Walter Citrine reviewed the alternative principles of craft, class, occupational, federal and industrial unionism, and pointed out how the undignified competition for members, exacerbated by varying rates of union contributions and benefit, demarcation disputes between crafts and lack of co-ordinated policy, obstructed 'scientific functioning' against capitalism.[3]

[1] V. L. Allen. *Power in Trade Unions.* 1954. For a brief sketch of these and other problems discussed in this section, see P. Ford. *Economics of Modern Industry.* 1930. pp. 159–92.

[2] Trades Union Congress, Scarborough, 1925. Rep. p. 229.

[3] T.U.C., Scarborough, 1925. Rep. pp. 226–37. Appendix B to the Memo. contains a list of resolutions of T.U.C. on the matter from 1874 onwards. On the great difficulties in collective bargaining caused by complicated bargaining units, see *The Press*, R. Com. Rep. paras. 99–108; 1961–62 Cmnd. 1811.

The 'amalgamation movement' did greatly reduce the number of unions and *pari passu* also led to the formation of some very large ones. The desire to remove competition for members, to add to union bargaining prestige by size and to express the solidarity of the workers—the One Big Union motive—all played their part. In V. L. Allen's view, growth in size occurred mainly because bigger units were more economical, could offer a wider range of specialist services, etc.; in a word, were more efficient.[1] In a movement beginning in 1917, three unions in the iron and steel trades surrendered to a Central Association (British Iron, Steel and Kindred Trades Association) the function of enrolling new members and to the Iron and Steel Trades Confederation questions of wages, conditions and the conduct of negotiations. The Transport and General Workers' Union had been built up out of various unions of dock workers, carters, bus and tramworkers, long-distance road transport men and taxi-drivers, as well as including trades as varied as Co-operative Insurance Society employees and a large number of general workers in varied industries; and its membership of $1\frac{1}{4}$ million was 16 per cent of the total membership affiliated to the Trades Union Congress.[2] The N.U.R. was an amalgamation and extension of three unions, the National Union of General and Municipal Workers of a number of 'general' unions. So that whereas in 1927 the number of unions affiliated to Congress was 205, with a membership of 4,164,000, in 1962 there were 182 affiliated unions with 8,312,000 members.

But Congress has made far less progress in achieving its aim of securing reorganization on the basis of industrial unionism. Existing craft unions did not wish to lose their identity and feared that their craftsmen's interests might not be as well looked after if they merged with unions having a dominantly unskilled membership. 'General unions' catering for general workers employed in a large number of different industries would have had to go out of existence,[3] and since many such workers move from industry to

[1] V. L. Allen. op. cit., pp. 21–2. The occurrence of damaging demarcation disputes was an important factor in stimulating the merger between the Boilermakers and the Shipwrights.

[2] For the history of this remarkable achievement, see F. Williams. *Ernest Bevin.* 1952. J. Goldstein. *The Government of British Trade Unions.* 1952. B. Tillett. *Memories and Reflections.* 1931. Chaps. XI, XIV. B. Tillett. *History of the London Transport Workers' Strike.* 1911.

[3] T.U.C., Brighton, 1946. Rep.

industry in the course of their employment, it could be claimed that they needed their own union to protect their special interests. There were also differences between unions regarding questions of policy for their industry. The more technical difficulties arising from differences of financial strength, in scales of contributions and benefit, could no doubt be overcome if the other obstacles were removed and there were a real will to amalgamate.[1] Faced with these difficulties, at the Brighton meeting, 1963, the General Council announced its intention of trying to promote groupings and mergers through extensive discussions with unions in which, if necessary, it would put forward its own suggestions.[2]

The outstanding case is that of the railways. The claim of the N.U.R. to be an industrial union negotiating for a proper and sensible 'wages structure' for the various grades of the industry, or to be an 'employment' union including in its membership all those working for a common employer, has point in that the demand for their labour and their pay are derived either from the demand for and the proceeds of the sale of a common final product, or from the sales of a common employer.[3] The object of an employment union 'must therefore be to have the power to withdraw the whole of the labour employed by a given group of employers, so that not only is profit-making prevented, but actual losses, due to the depreciation of capital . . . and administrative charges, are inflicted to a maximum on the employers . . . the union must have control of the whole of the workers employed by these employers'.[4] An industrial union has an economic reason to commend it in addition to any support which may be derived from those ideals of 'workers' control', 'industrial democracy' or 'guild socialism' which have sometimes been regarded as peculiarly applicable to this industry. Either basis of organization has carried with it the claim by the N.U.R. that the men in the railway workshops,[5] on the 'railway steamships' and the railway hotels 'belong' to them. But this cuts across the equally

[1] *Trade Union Structure and Closer Unity.* T.U.C., 1947. Approved by Brighton Congress, 1946. See also T.U.C. Reports, 1944–47.

[2] See speech by Woodcock, T.U.C., Sept. 2nd, 1963.

[3] These two different conceptions seem to have been confused by the N.U.R. 'The N.U.R. claimed that their union is an industrial union catering for all men employed by the railway companies.' T.U.C., Hull, 1924. Rep. pp. 155–6.

[4] T.U.C., Scarborough, 1925. Rep. p. 233.

[5] 'The Organization of Railway Shopmen.' In, T.U.C., Scarborough, 1925. Rep. pp. 210–13. Also Report of Hull Congress, 1924. p. 149.

strong claims of other unions that the men on railway ships are not landlubbers, but seamen, whose pay should be related to that of other seamen and not that of land transport workers,[1] and that the pay of the engineers and other craftsmen in railway workshops should be related to that of fellow craftsmen performing the same operations as themselves in other industries;[2] it is the market for their craft as a whole which should be taken into account. And even if all industries were organized on a 'guild' basis, this would still have point. An Industrial Court award on the wages of railway shopmen made in 1922, in which the Court decided, in effect, that their employment by the railway was more relevant than their craft[3] did not settle this dispute, which was the subject of an unsuccessful intervention by T.U.C. in 1925. The real and longstanding difficulties are, however, amongst workers on the railways proper, between the N.U.R. (which includes station staff, platelayers, signalmen, guards, etc.), the Associated Society of Locomotive Engineers and Firemen and the Transport Salaried Staffs Association (Railway Clerks Association), each representing in the main different grades. The two latter unions apparently have been willing to consider joint working arrangements, but the N.U.R. was said to be interested in fusion only.[4]

Concluding from difficulties such as these that full and universal industrial unionism was unrealistic,[5] following the precedent of individual pioneer experiments, Congress tried to improve bargaining strength by encouraging 'federation', in which the unions retain

[1] National Sailors' and Firemen's Union v. National Union of Railwaymen. T.U.C., Hull, 1924. Rep. pp. 155–6. 'I should like to know what a railwayman knows about the load line on ships.' Mr. Cathery, N.S.F.U. p. 299.

[2] See United Pattern Makers' Association v. National Union of Railwaymen. T.U.C., Hull, 1924. Rep. p. 149. On the whole question see W. Citrine's memo on *Organization by Industry.* Report of Scarborough Congress, 1925. pp. 226–40. But see the decision on a complaint of the Transport and General Workers' Union on the position of locomen employed by Swansea Harbour Trust when this was merged with the Great Western Railway. Hull Congress Report. p. 141.

[3] Industrial Court Award No. 728. *Railway Shopmen.* paras. 7–12, 16–17. July 1922. See W. Milne-Bailey. *Trade Union Documents.* 1929. pp. 279–84.

[4] *Trade Union Structure and Closer Unity.* 1947. p. 18. See also T.U.C., Blackpool, 1957. Rep. pp. 335–6.

[5] Ibid. See replies of unions, pp. 18–19, and T.U.C., 1957 Report, Tewson's speech, pp. 337–8. See also Interim Report on *Trade Union Structure and Closer Unity.* In, T.U.C., Blackpool, 1944. Rep. p. 341 *et seq.*

autonomy but co-ordinate their policy on economic questions, and joint working arrangements.[1] Why they should do this was obvious enough when there appeared on negotiating committees or wages councils representatives of different unions each claiming to speak for the same class or group of workpeople,[2] with the risk that they might sometimes pursue different policies. A number of unions have set up national joint committees or made joint working arrangements, and these may be developed up to the point of 'federation'.

The T.U.C. had before it two obvious examples of 'federation'. The Confederation of Shipbuilding and Engineering Unions is an organization of some forty unions, each maintaining its own separate union identity and organization. Eighty per cent of the members belong to seven large unions—half a million to the Amalgamated Engineering Union, over 150,000 to the Foundry Workers, Electrical Trades Union and Draughtsmen, while 200,000, mainly labourers, are members of two general unions, either the Transport and General Workers or the National Union of General and Municipal Workers, which have many members in other industries. The Confederation has its own internal problems of the balance of power between larger and small unions and of the relationship between craftsmen and labourers, but has two negotiating committees, one for shipbuilding and one for engineering.

The two general unions are also represented in the National Federation of Building Trade Operatives. This Federation differs from that of the Shipbuilding and Engineering Unions in that while the affiliated unions retain their separate identity, the Federation has its own full-time regional offices, determines industrial policy and may without consultation call members of affiliated unions out on strike locally. The separate unions remain responsible for the strike pay of their own members involved, but receive a per head payment from the Federation.

These attempts to create 'industrial' bargaining units, whether in the form of industrial unions or in industrial 'federations' are not

[1] Even securing between four unions uniformity of contributions of certain classes of local government employees would involve within the unions which have members in other industries different rates of contributions for the same benefits. T.U.C., Blackpool, 1962, p. 108. Portsmouth, 1961, pp. 216–18.

[2] For example, three tobacco workers' unions and three general unions on the Tobacco Wages Board. See *Trade Union Structure and Closer Unity*. p. 45. See speech by Chapple. T.U.C., Brighton, 1963. Sept. 2nd.

without their own difficulties. Despite the problems of organization connected with railway shopmen and railway-owned ships, it is not difficult to think of railway transport as an 'industry': the railways are a single financial unit, selling a transport service. But what is the engineering industry? It really consists of a wide series of industries making products as different as motor cars, household appliances, textile machinery, machine tools, etc., and engines of all kinds, some of which may be prosperous at the same time as others are in difficulties. The sales proceeds from which wages are paid come from quite different markets: the situation is therefore different from that in a clearly defined single-product or single-service industry, where the difference between firms is one of efficiency, and union pressure for a high rate may help the efficient as against the inefficient firm. It is conceivable that better basic rates could be obtained for those engineering industries which are prosperous by bargaining for them separately, instead of including them in a uniform national agreement. This problem of industrial boundary can crop up sharply during a strike, as it did in 1957. Most manufacturing industries employ engineers, if only for maintenance. Thus engineers were called out in the rubber industry, on the Manchester Canal and in cable making, thereby creating tensions with other unions whose members were put off work though they had no connection with the dispute and had separate negotiating machinery. In addition, the affiliated unions have separate rates of contribution, and separate rates of strike pay, some more generous than others, their financial reserves vary, and some have obligations to members in other industries.[1]

At its inception the unions represented in the T.U.C. were in the main organizations of skilled and unskilled manual workers, but since 1918 there has been a remarkable and significant growth of unions and associations at all levels of wage and salary earning. Their membership includes professional, technical, administrative and supervisory workers, such as teachers, civil servants, local government officers, actors, scientific workers, university lecturers,

[1] The effect of this on the management and termination of the engineering strike of 1957 is very clearly brought out in H. A. Clegg and R. Adams. *The Employers' Challenge*. 1957. pp. 110–12, 115–20. The book gives a detailed and clear analysis.

etc., whose maximum incomes, reached, say, in the 'middle years', may be above or far above those of the manual workers. Some are associations of more or less self-contained professions, such as teachers, who have only a minute number of manual workers, such as caretakers, in their 'industry', while others of these groups are in posts of responsibility, in authority over manual workers who are members of other unions. Some of the bodies are registered as trade unions, and others are not; some are affiliated to the T.U.C., but others are not affiliated and not subject to its jurisdiction or official influence. But even when they are neither registered nor affiliated, they may negotiate wages and represent their members on wage-determining bodies in much the same way as registered and affiliated unions. The growth of these unions and associations catering for the upper levels of salary earning has introduced a new and important factor into collective bargaining viewed as a whole. Whether these unions or associations should affiliate to T.U.C., as some have done, or build up some form of central 'white collar' organization, such as the Federation of Professional Workers, into something like a separate trade union congress, as in Sweden, is still a subject of debate.

The organizations which have been described may conduct their bargaining either directly with the employers, or by using formal machinery, such as the joint industrial councils established in many industries since the Whitley Report on the *Relations of Employers and Employed*, 1917, for this and other purposes. In some industries, such as engineering, the two 'sides' are apt to meet only when a wage claim is made and thus when a possible dispute is looming up. But Joint Industrial Councils not only deal with questions such as welfare, recruitment, training and grading of staff, on which there may be co-operation between the parties, but have the advantage of regular meetings, some at least of which have no air of a pending dispute about them. Though they are important in the contribution they make to industrial relations, there is no need here for any detailed examination of them. For bargaining, with which we are concerned, takes place just the same, even if in a better atmosphere, and it is open to the worker's side, for example, unable to get its wage claim accepted, to carry the matter to the industrial court; and some have done so.

2. RECOGNITION

The recognition by the employers of the right of their workers, not only to join but to be represented by a union and by an 'outside' union officer not in their own employ has long been won by the craft and other older trade societies. The commendation of collective bargaining by the Industrial Council in 1913 was strengthened in 1919 by the Industrial Conference, a large body representative of employers and employed. It reaffirmed that negotiating machinery should be established, with full acceptance of employers' organizations and trade unions as recognized bodies able to act on behalf of their members, and that 'members should accept the jurisdiction of their respective organizations'.[1] The General Strike of 1926 caused a temporary setback, for many men in various industries left their work on a matter—miners' wages—not within the purview or the responsibility of their own employers, and this greatly exacerbated industrial relations in certain industries, even in firms and industries in which unions had been fully recognized. But in 1928 there was an even more explicit statement. A conference of the 'Mond' group of employers and the T.U.C. General Council in a joint resolution stated that industry had so greatly benefited by the progressive increase in the volume of joint negotiation and by the growth of various forms of joint machinery, that this ought to be encouraged and extended, and that it was 'to the interests of all concerned that full recognition should be given to bona fide trade unions'. Like the Industrial Council earlier, it considered that negotiations were facilitated if workers and employers were members of their respective organizations.[2] Refusal to 'recognize' a trade union would now be regarded as anachronistic, one recent example being itself a heritage of the General Strike.[3] The difficulties experienced by white-collar unions in banking and insurance in securing recognition even where the majority of employees are members, are due to the preference of the banks and some of the staffs for 'house' unions. This preference is said to arise from banks' dislike

[1] *Industrial Conference.* Rep. p. 10; 1919 Cmd. 501, xxiv. (Report only; 1919 Cmd. 139, xxiv)

[2] W. Milne-Bailey. *Trade Union Documents.* pp. 460–1.

[3] *D. C. Thomson & Co. Ltd. and ... NATSOPA. Dispute.* Ct. of Inquiry. Rep.; 1951–52 Cmd. 8607, xv.

of the unions' affiliation to the T.U.C., which might advocate policies affecting industries in which their clients are engaged.[1]

3. BARGAINING RIGHTS, THE UNION SHOP AND THE CLOSED SHOP

But a good deal more was involved in the full general acceptance of the principle of recognition than was at first evident. On the union side, what were the respective 'bargaining rights' of various trade unions each with members in a plant? We have seen how as unions swarmed into the unoccupied fields, the need arose to prevent 'poaching' and to determine which union had the 'right to organize' particular groups of workers, but this in due course often developed into the larger question as to which union or unions possessed 'the bargaining rights' or even 'exclusive bargaining rights' for the men or works in question. In a dispute between the National Union of Blastfurnacemen and the Iron and Steel Trades Confederation, the former claimed 'the right to organize and negotiate for all the men concerned with the operation of the blast furnaces'.[2] In various cases the National Union of General and Municipal Workers claimed 'the organizational prerogative' as against the Confederation of Health Service Employees, the National Union of Printing, Bookbinding and Paper Workers and the Sign and Display Trade Union.[3] T.U.C. Disputes Committees' decisions on these and other cases took account not simply of the best principles of trade union organization (on which it had spent much time) and of the nature of the work on which the men concerned were engaged, but also of which union was 'in first', which had most members at the relevant date, etc. T.U.C. has also allocated different rayon works between three different unions,[4] and arranged spheres of influence, some industrial, some geographical; e.g. workers in hotels, restaurants, cafés, in London and South-Western counties have been assigned to N.U.G.M.W., those in North-Western, North Midland and North Welsh counties to the N.U.D.A.W. and those in East Anglia, East Midlands and North-Eastern counties to the Shop Assistants.[5] In works which employ

[1] T.U.C., Douglas, 1960. Rep. pp. 341–4. Portsmouth, 1961, Rep. p. 121.
[2] T.U.C., Blackpool, 1957. Rep. p. 97.
[3] Ibid. pp. 101, 106, 109.
[4] *Trade Union Structure and Closer Unity*. T.U.C., 1947. p. 20.
[5] Ibid. p. 66.

tiers of crafts and grades of workers, such decisions may give a
union the bargaining rights on behalf of some grade or grades only;
but in other works with but a limited number of grades these may
amount to 'exclusive bargaining rights'. Sometimes such exclusive
bargaining rights may be given to a union by the employer: the
London Passenger Transport Board to the Transport and General
Workers' Union in 1946[1] in respect of certain workers. But the
Electrical Trades Union failed in a claim before the Court of
Inquiry to exclusive bargaining rights for certain branches of the
work of the London Electricity Board which was opposed by other
unions.[2] Sometimes an employer, on his own initiative or under
pressure from established unions, may express his reluctance to
deal with minority unions. The Postmaster-General, faced with
thirty-one unions, said that recognition would be considered only
if a union had 40 per cent of the membership of its grade and would
be withdrawn if this fell below $33\frac{1}{3}$ per cent. But later the Terrington
Committee recommended the withdrawal of this principle and
placing on any union claiming recognition the onus of proving that
it served its members better than an existing organization—by
implication claiming the right to select between unions which, if
made by a private employer, would not have passed without
criticism.[3]

How much is now implied on the employer's side by 'recognition'? In many industries it has clearly gone beyond permitting or
encouraging employees to join trade unions: is it to mean that all
workers *have* to join a union, though a union of their own choice
(a 'union shop'), or that they must joint a *particular* union, as a
condition of being given or retained in employment? It will be seen
that the latter course means both conferring exclusive bargaining
rights on a particular union and compulsory unionism. And an
employer's agreement to make employment conditional on the
worker joining some union of his own choice might in practice be
turned by trade union amalgamations or inter-union arrangements
giving one of them exclusive organizational rights into compulsory

[1] H. A. Clegg. *Labour Relations in London Transport.* 1950. p. 37.
[2] *Electrical T.U. and the London Electricity Bd. Dispute.* Ct. of Inquiry.
Rep. paras. 11, 13; 1950–51 Cmd. 8232, xvi.
[3] *Post Office (Departmental Classes) Recognition.* Cttee. Rep.; 1951–52
Cmd. 8470, xviii. See P. and G. Ford. *Breviate of Parliamentary Papers 1940–
1954,* pp. 217–18.

membership of a particular union.[1] In any case, not only do some unions—particularly craft unions—lay on the members an obligation to refuse to work with non-unionists if instructed by the union to do so, but the feeling of dislike of non-unionists may be so great that even though technically free to join or not to join a union, or any particular union, for the non-unionist life in the workshop would be intolerable unless he did so. 'Recognition' has thus come to mean in practice a great deal more than appears to have been contemplated either in 1912 or 1919.

4. DISCIPLINE AND FULFILMENT OF AGREEMENTS

The Report on *Industrial Agreements* referred to 'the difficulty of ascertaining beforehand the exact wishes of those represented'[2] as one reason why agreements were sometimes not honoured. The unions' rank and file look in the pay packet to see what has actually been secured, but it is the union leader who has conducted negotiations with the employers who knows what the difficulties have been and who may sometimes have to come near to arguing part of the employer's case when justifying a concession he has had to make. But besides this difficulty, general to all trade union bargaining, there are three others of importance. The first arises from the enlargement of unions. By the inclusion of workers of different grades of skill, etc., the internal pressures within unions are increased, for the question is how the gains of collective bargaining are to be distributed amongst the different trades and groups of

---

[1] The National Society of Metal Mechanics complained that its members had difficulty in finding employment because of other unions' closed shop policy. T.U.C., Blackpool, 1962, p. 40. T.U.C. Special Report on *The Closed Shop*, 1946, is not completely consistent. It emphasizes that 100 per cent unionism is the trade union objective, that it does not recognize the right of a workman to be free to join a trade union or not as he pleases (p. 6). But it says also that the 'closed shop' in the sense of 'an establishment in which only members of a particular union can be employed to the exclusion of members of other unions, is alien to British trade union practice and theory'. What it means by this is that it 'has never consented to the recognition of an exclusive right to organize by one union where other unions have built up their organization side by side' (p. 5). If, however, it were successful in promoting one union for each industry, e.g. on the railways, and refused affiliation to any breakaway union, from the point of view of the individual workman, the industry would be not only a 'union shop' but a 'closed shop'.

[2] Rep. p. 4; 1913 Cd. 6952, xxviii.

workers concerned: whether, for example, the differential between loco drivers, signalmen and station staff, or between London and provincial bus workers should be decreased, maintained or increased.[1] To meet these strains, the strengthening of central control has sometimes been accompanied by striking and ingenious arrangements for giving the different trade groups constitutional expression, e.g. the T.G.W.U. is organized into fourteen trade groups and thirteen areas. But even this combination of central control and trade autonomy, though in the main efficient, has not always been easy to work, for the union has not been able to avoid either some unofficial and breakaway movements amongst dockers, or a dissident bus workers' organization. The long series of difficulties with dockers includes a strike against an agreement in 1924, which led to the formation of a small union which later became the National Amalgamated Stevedores, Lightermen, Watermen and Dockers' Union;[2] trouble with Glasgow dockers, who eventually formed a separate union for that area only; later trouble with the stevedores in Manchester and Liverpool, and unofficial strikes spread from port to port by active unofficial emissaries. And there was an unofficial rank-and-file movement amongst London bus workers in the inter-war years, and a rival National Passenger Workers' Union in the provinces. Sometimes the differences have been due to the dislike of an agreement, or to long negotiating procedures, sometimes to the insistence of the unions in keeping an agreement even if its terms were violently disliked (such as compulsory overtime in the docks). The union has had to use a mixture of understanding, so that dissidents should not be driven into extreme breakaway movements, and of firmness, such as insistence that officers should sign a declaration and even suffer expulsion.[3] The N.U.R. constitution also provides for the representation of sectional interests, but the majority of loco men remain outside it in the A.S.L.E.F.[4] While no doubt the support given by affiliated unions to T.U.C. action against breakaway unions—even though such organizations might sometimes be the only and final form of protest against their union's policy or management left open to dissenting members—may not

[1] Industrial Disputes Tribunal. Award No. 1006. 1957. pp. 4–5.
[2] V. L. Allen. *Trade Union Leadership*. 1957. p. 59.
[3] Ibid. p. 70.
[4] T.U.C., Blackpool, 1957. Rep. p. 336. Debate, Hallworth, 75,000 out of 82,000.

be entirely uninfluenced by the natural desire of established bodies to hamper new rivals, it is in fact implied by the stable conditions needed for successful collective bargaining. It is this which explains its insistence on the observance of the 'Bridlington Rules' for avoiding 'poaching' of members,[1] especially if there is any suspicion of a breakaway movement. It directed the National Amalgamated Stevedores and Dockers' Union to return members to the Transport and General Workers' Union, and after an adverse High Court decision had created some difficulties, suspended its affiliation for not obeying its instructions.[2] There is clearly room for embarrassment if a breakaway union insists on conducting parallel or separate negotiations and it is natural that an established union should resist its being represented on a joint board with employers. There was a long struggle, including a strike, by the stevedores for representation on the Merseyside Dock Labour Joint Committee.[3] The established union may treat members of a breakaway union as non-unionists and decline to work with them; and an employer may decide to dismiss them.[4]

Secondly, there may also be some tension and conflict between the central and higher and the local and lower levels of leadership found in the branches and amongst the shop stewards, as well as between the national officers and the rank and file. Sometimes shop stewards are appointed by a union, or they may be elected by all the men in the workshop irrespective of their particular union. Their functions may include the collection of dues and taking up local workshop matters with the management. They are in the place where troubles begin—the workshop—and their power has probably been somewhat increased as national have replaced district wage agreements, by the length of time which a difficult point in dispute

[1] T.U.C., Bridlington, 1939. Rep. Sections 19–24.

[2] T.U.C., Southport, 1955. Rep. pp. 106–17. Brighton, 1956. pp. 99–101. Blackpool, 1957. pp. 117–19. Blackpool, 1959. pp. 110–15, 326–28. There was an early struggle between the National Union of Seamen and the British Seafarers' Union. See T.U.C. reports, 1924–25, and B. Mogridge, *Militancy and Inter-Union Rivalries in British Shipping*, International Review of Social History, 1961. For an instructive study of three cases see Shirley W. Lerner, *Breakaway Unions and Small Trade Unions*, 1961.

[3] *Port Transport Industry*. Cttee. Rep. p. 13; 1955–56 Cmd. 9813, xxvi.

[4] As in the case of 36 members of the National Association of Toolmakers. *Times*, Sept. 7th, 1963, p. 8e.

takes to pass from the local to the national level for settlement, and by the increased opportunities for local gains in conditions of full employment. Nor have they to take into account the wider issues, as do the national officers responsible for negotiating and securing the implementations of national agreements. Many unofficial strikes and unofficial, internal union troubles have begun with them.

If stewards are not appointed by the unions, but elected by the workshop, the majority of men may belong to one union and the steward to another with only a few members in that workshop. In such cases the control of the unions over the shop steward is weak. They have little over joint committees of shop stewards in one workplace, none over committees linking joint committees in several factories under common ownership ('Combine stewards committees'), or over national shop steward's movements not limited to any one industry. It is these bodies which have been so closely associated with unofficial strikes in breach of agreements, defiance of union policies or a union's specific instruction. Such strikes have caused inter-union friction because they have indirectly put out of work members of unions which have not been consulted in accordance with the principles emphasized by T.U.C. and have even involved unions in dispute pay in a matter not of their seeking.[1] In one firm the shop stewards were able to act independently of the union by financing their activities from a completely independent fund of £16,000, less £9,000 in prizes, raised by the sale of lottery (pools) tickets, the remainder being regarded as the sinews of war.[2] It is clearly possible, in a great works like Ford's at Dagenham, employing 30,000 people who are members of a number of different unions, if there is no one permanent officer of a national union looking after the working of disputes and consultation procedure, and stewards are elected by the floor on a show of hands and not by ballot, for a determined militant group to turn the shop steward's organization to its own account.[3]

[1] T.U.C., Douglas. Rep. 1960. Speech by Williamson, p. 353.

[2] *Briggs Motor Bodies, Ltd., Dagenham. Dispute.* Ct. of Inquiry. Rep.; 1956–57 Cmnd. 131, xiv.

[3] *Dispute between the Ford Motor Company Ltd., Dagenham, and Members of the Trade Unions. . . .* Ct. of Inquiry. Rep.; 1962–63 Cmnd. 1999. Especially paras. 105–8, 127–33.

In an analysis of the problem in *Disputes and Workshop Organization*[1] the General Council of the T.U.C. emphasized the positive work of the 200,000 shop stewards in industry in settling local disputes peacefully and the widespread use of joint committees in works. But it clearly could not countenance an alternative movement or any body trying to encroach on the unions' policy-making function, and prompted a little, perhaps, by rising public hostility and whispers about restrictive legislation, declared that members' participation in such bodies was contrary to their obligations to their unions. Some of these difficulties may be due to the fact that English unions have been based traditionally on an area branch, rather than on a workshop basis: i.e. the workshop and shop stewards are not always drawn into or made the basis of union organization. The discussion amongst the trade unionists during the years 1917–20 on workshop versus branch organization, which arose out of the shop stewards' movements in World War I was thus not without its point[2] though the persistence of branch organization can scarcely be due merely to conservatism. It remains to be seen whether the new pressures arising out of full employment, which have created fresh opportunities for local bargaining and shop stewards' activities, may not eventually require controlled devolution of some powers to the local units.

Unrealistic wage claims and the rejection of union officers' advice arise partly from this source. The tens of thousands of rank and file of a large union cannot be expected to go into the details of a complicated wage settlement and negotiations must be and are in the main carried on by their representatives unhampered. Nor can they be expected to know or even be aware of the things which the union officer picks up during his discussions with employers, such as the financial strength and weakness of different firms, their detailed difficulties, contracts in the export market offered and lost, trade prospects, etc. It is thus possible for them to formulate quite unrealistic demands, which if granted could have serious economic consequences which they do not perceive. Thus the engineers rejected the advice of their officers that their demands were

[1] T.U.C., Douglas. Rep. 1960., pp. 124–6, 329–33, 346–53, 356–8.
[2] J. T. Murphy. *The Unit of Organization: Branch* v. *Workshop.* In, *The Trade Unions: Organization and Action.* Publ. by the Council of Ruskin College, Oxford. 1919. Mr. Murphy was Chairman of the Sheffield Shop Stewards' Committee. See the comments of Small and Speak, pp. 23, 26.

C

unrealistic, busmen rejected advice not to separate the demands of London and provincial busmen into separate claims. The criticisms sometimes passed on the men for rejecting the advice of their 'leaders' are often misconceived, because they are based on authoritarian assumptions out of place in trade union constitutions; the officers are elected by and are the servants of the members, who are entitled to give them their instructions. The various union constitutions try to solve the problem of who shall finally decide the acceptance of proposed terms of settlement in varied ways. Sometimes the union executive has full powers and its decisions are binding on its members, while in others the decision requires the sanction of a delegate conference, which is free to accept or reject. Difficulties of this kind are a natural occurrence in any attempt to arrive at wage decisions by democratic processes. But it has to be remembered that unrealistic claims may be made also as part of the bargaining process, for otherwise there would be no explanation for the readiness with which compromise figures substantially less than claims are so often accepted. According to Peacock and Ryan, settlements at one-half to two-thirds of claim figures were commonly accepted in 1948–50.[1]

Thirdly, how far is any 'difficulty of ascertaining beforehand the exact wishes of those represented' due to the limited proportion of members who participate actively in union policy making and government? In 1954 only 10 per cent of the members of the A.E.U. voted in the election of the president.[2] In 1953, 40,000 E.T.U. members were affected by a dispute; seventeen mass meetings were held, and 2,617, or 6 per cent, attended and voted.[3] One of the difficulties in the dispute at the Austin works was that 'workers would not stay for meetings after working hours because of the distance they had to travel'.[4] Mr. Goldstein pointed out that on an average only 37 per cent of the members voted for elections to the General Executive Council of the T.G.W.U. and 35 per cent to 38 per cent for the election of the General Secretary, while only

[1] A. T. Peacock and W. J. L. Ryan. 'Wage Claims and the Pace of Inflation.' *Economic Journal*, June 1953. pp. 385–92.

[2] *The Times.* Feb. 24th, 1954. p. 8f.

[3] *National Federated Electrical Assoc. and the Electrical T.U. Dispute.* Ct. of Inquiry. Rep. p. 11; 1952–53 Cmd. 8968, xiii.

[4] *Austin Motor Co. Ltd. and . . . National Union of Vehicle Builders. Dispute.* Ct. of Inquiry. Rep.; 1952–53 Cmd. 8839, xiii.

4 per cent to 7 per cent attended branch meetings. Owing to the high proportion of members who were general labourers in the habit of migrating from industry to industry, the proportion of 'lapsed' members was one-third of the total, and nearly equal to the number of new members. This, together with the years of service at their respective trades required before a man could be eligible for office, meant that although 80 per cent of the members were eligible for benefit, 80 per cent were not eligible for office.[1] It was Goldstein's contention that this situation made it possible for a small active political, e.g. communist, group to exercise a decisive and possibly unrepresentative influence on elections. We are not here concerned with the possible consequences of such a political situation, with whether it squares with the presumptions of democratic theory, or in what circumstances and in what sense a minority or *élite* group can represent the views or wishes of the whole body of members, but only with the narrower question of what is the effect on the process of negotiation and fulfilment of agreements.

It is to be expected that if employment is conditional on holding a union card, i.e. if membership of a trade union is compulsory, there will be many members who go through the formality of membership for that reason and not because they are particularly interested in union business as such. An older trade unionist might point to the figures as confirmation of his view, which the present generation of active unionists do not share, that one voluntary trade unionist is worth two conscripts. The non-participation of members is therefore not just 'apathy', but is in part at least a natural consequence both of compulsory membership and of the creation of mass unions where the members cannot be closely knit. Such a situation is not, however, new. Forty years ago J. T. Murphy pointed out how low were percentages voting on twenty-eight different occasions in eleven unions.[2] In the A.E.U. election referred to above, voting was by branches and at that time only about 10 per cent of members attended branch meetings. Nor is the problem limited to trade unions, many other voluntary societies exhibiting the same characteristics. Only some 2 per cent of members of co-operative societies

[1] J. Goldstein. *The Government of British Trade Unions.* 1952.

[2] J. T. Murphy. op. cit. pp. 15, 16. 'To get an attendance of 70 or 100 out of a branch membership of 300 to 1,000 is a sign of stirring times or of unemployment. There are thousands of members who have rarely seen the inside of a branch room'—p. 14.

normally attend their annual meetings;[1] indeed, if they all tried to do so, most towns would not possess meeting halls big enough to hold the thousands of members. Various constitutional procedures, including postal ballots, have been tried in order to provide opportunities for at least some participation in major decisions. In fact, the sufficiency of the arrangements rests on the assumption that in matters of this kind the self-selected, active participating minority somehow broadly shares the attitude and reflects the wishes of their fellow members. In union matters this would seem to be confirmed by the general loyalty of members in carrying out decisions to strike. It is common for large numbers of members to turn up at decisive strike meetings, though they may not have attended meetings which led up to the strike situation. Nevertheless, sometimes the machinery creaks and the question is how significant these creaks are. The answer probably is, not very: they could be so only if the minority of participating members push a claim or programme far beyond what the ordinary non-active members were willing to support by strike action. There are clear limits to this, for even a disruptive political group could not in the long run gain much by engineering a strike unsuccessful because inadequately supported.[2]

5. A CODE OF INDUSTRIAL CONDUCT

The Industrial Council's report emphasized that the success of collective bargaining was due to a recognition by both sides of the moral obligations involved, and that moral influences should in every way be brought to bear in carrying out agreements strictly. If written twenty years later, it might have added that with the change of bargaining from a district to a national basis, success depended also on the observance of recognized processes and techniques of the negotiating process itself. The British industrial constitution, like its political constitution, has its unwritten conventions, and violation of them can cause serious difficulties. Thus

[1] A. M. Carr Saunders, P. S. Florence., R. Peers. *Consumers' Co-operation.* 1938. Pt. III. Fig. 31. This confirms the earlier analysis of the Webbs in *The Consumers' Co-operative Movement.* 1921. pp. 49, 305.

[2] The activities of a minority of members working legitimately and within the rules is quite different from the rigging of elections and falsification of votes which led the T.U.C. to expel the Electrical Trades Union. For the attitude and decisions of T.U.C. see Rep. Portsmouth, 1961, App. B, pp. 471 and 296–312; on re-admission, Blackpool, 1962, pp. 283–4.

the 1925 agreement between the Iron and Steel Trades Employers'
Association and the National Union of General and Municipal
Workers tried to set out in writing the recognized processes which
had been built up by custom and practice, and these included, for
example, no stoppage of work during negotiations, and no negotiations whilst men were on strike. That is, chances of settlement
should not be diminished by placing either side under duress during
discussions. An even more vital rule is that a union should not be
asked to agree to a reduction of wages prior to and as a condition
of commencing negotiations. The owners—and the Government—
did in 1926, following the Samuel Commission's report, ask the
miners to accept the principle of a reduction before commencing
negotiations. The miners refused, and Mr. J. H. Thomas, of the
railwaymen, though later severely criticized for his part in the
General Strike, protested hotly that this request was a complete
violation of negotiating practice and struck at the root of collective
bargaining.[1] But the rule works both ways. The Electrical Trades
Union demanded that the employers' association (National Federated Electrical Association) should agree to part of the increase of
wages claimed, and should recommend their branches to that effect,
leaving only the remainder of the increase to be negotiated. The
employers refused. Similarly, the Court commented adversely on
the N.U.R's action in trying to insist that the Transport Commission
should concede a substantial part of their claim as a condition of
further negotiation.[2] During a dispute the E.T.U. called token
strikes on the sites, not only of some employers and not others, but
of employers who were on the negotiating committee. On this the
Industrial Court laid it down that it was fundamental that people
who took part in negotiations representing their sides should do so
in the knowledge that their personal position would not be preju-
diced. This is, of course, only the reverse side of the rule that no
worker should be victimized for representing the employees or the
union.[3] Calling a meeting of the men in Austin Motor Company's

[1] *The Mining Crisis and the National Strike 1926.* T.U.C., 1927. Report of
Mr. Thomas' speech. p. 30. The same point was made, less plainly, by Mr.
Pugh. p. 28.
[2] *British Transport Com. and the N.U.R. Dispute.* Ct. of Inquiry. Final Rep.
paras. 20, 51; 1954–55 Cmd. 9372, v.
[3] *National Federated Electrical Assoc. and the Electrical T.U. Dispute.* Ct. of
Inquiry. Rep. pp. 12, 17, 21; 1952–53 Cmd. 8968, xiii.

works during working hours was regarded by the Court of Inquiry as a breach of an agreement that no stoppage should occur until the agreed procedure had been gone through.[1] One feature of a dispute between the London Electricity Board and the Electrical Trades Union was that, in trying to assert its claim to sole negotiating rights, the union had accepted as a member one of the Transport and General Workers' Union's members without consulting it or going through Disputes Committee of T.U.C. The Court affirmed that the union should have gone through the proper procedure laid down by T.U.C. and that the London Electricity Board was ill-advised to intervene on that point.[2] Some of the provincial bus companies claimed the right to withdraw from arbitration on a national agreement after matters had been taken through the Association to a national level. The Court thought this ill-advised and contrary to practice. It was essential to the operation of voluntary collective bargaining that application for revision of agreements or accepted standards which were national in character should be dealt with on a national basis.[3] The Court rebuked the Iron and Steel Trades Employers' Association for being rigid and intransigent on meeting the maintenance craftsmen's difficulties on procedure, and the craftsmen's unions for resort to an overtime embargo and striking against the employers' use of emergency maintenance teams.[4] The National Amalgamated Stevedores and Dockers were reproved for a ban or stoppage of overtime and a withdrawal of labour in breach of conciliation arrangements and the National Joint Council constitution.[5]

Fundamental to the code is the acceptance by all parties of the principle that signed agreements must be honoured. It is certain that the alternative suggestion in the Report on *Industrial Agreements* that such agreements should be legally enforceable would now be rejected by the unions as a grave restriction on their liberty.

[1] *Austin Motor Co. Ltd. and . . . National Union of Vehicle Builders. Dispute.* Ct. of Inquiry. Rep. p. 12; 1952–53 Cmd. 8839, xiii.

[2] *Electrical T.U. and the London Electricity Bd. Dispute.* Ct. of Inquiry. Rep. p. 13; 1950–51 Cmd. 8232, xvi.

[3] *National Council for the Omnibus Industry. Dispute.* Ct. of Inquiry. Rep. pp. 16–17; 1953–54 Cmd. 9093, xv.

[4] *Iron and Steel Trades Employers' Assoc. and the National Jt. Trade Unions' Craftsmen's Iron and Steel Cttee. Dispute.* Ct. of Inquiry. Rep. paras. 76, 78; 1955–56 Cmd. 9843, xxi.

[5] *London Docks. Dispute.* Ct. of Inquiry. Final Rep. para. 62, xi, xii; 1953–54 Cmd. 9310, xv.

But it is not always easy to honour agreements. Circumstances may change and undermine their basis, most agreements are compromises and somebody may be hurt or disappointed by their terms. In spite of these difficulties, union officers have consistently and firmly taken the line with disaffected members that agreements must be respected. Under both Bevin and Deakin the T.G.W.U. lost members to rival bodies for insistence upon it. Nevertheless, this does not mean that in no case will a union or its officers consent to break an agreement, for they may be presented with a choice between that and having the union impaired by breakaway or disruptive movements. The National Union of Printing, Book-binding and Paper Workers was sharply rebuked by the Court of Inquiry into the Thomson dispute for breaking agreements with three associations—the papermakers, the London and the provincial distributors—although they were not directly concerned, in order to inflict loss on that firm in the hope that it would lead to its agreeing to undertake collective bargaining. The Secretary told the Court that while he was anxious to honour agreements, the resentment in this case was so deep that he was not prepared to use ordinary trade union discipline to keep the men in, and that in the clash of loyalties he chose the major one. This did not, however, satisfy the Court.[1] Frequent unofficial strikes in breach of agreements have raised doubts on whether the sanctity attached to them has declined. The Devlin Committee, recording a long list of disputes of this kind in the ports, concluded that the unions had made sincere efforts to work the Port of London Scheme and its procedures, but that in the peculiar history and circumstances of dock labour there was no easy remedy for mass indiscipline. But the Lloyd-Williams Committee condemned the London Ocean Steamship Owners' Tally Clerks for a damaging unofficial strike, and the Jack Report on the disputes at Fords, Dagenham, commented adversely on the unions' failure to deal with the unofficial organization connected with them, as they had been urged to do in the Cameron Report six years earlier.[2]

[1] D. C. Thomson & Co. Ltd. and . . . NATSOPA. Dispute. Ct. of Inquiry. Rep. pp. 34–5 and para. 149; 1951–52 Cmd. 8607, xv.
[2] Port Transport Industry. Cttee. Rep. paras. 24–6, 88; 1955–56 Cmd. 9813, xxvi. Ocean Shipowners' Tally Clerks, Cttee. Rep. pp. 14–15; 1960. Non-Parl. Dispute between the Ford Motor Company Ltd., Dagenham, and Members of the Trade Unions. . . . Ct. of Inquiry. Rep. paras. 127–9; 1962–63 Cmnd. 1999.

6. COLLECTIVE BARGAINING BY PROXY

Over a considerable part of the field, covering a fifth of all the wage-earners, collective bargaining may be said to take place by proxy, through the machinery of Wages Councils. In industries and trades in which neither trade unions nor sometimes employers have been able to organize effectively, there were only rudimentary means of finding out the wishes of those concerned and no means of ensuring that an agreement would be kept by persons not signatories to it. These two difficulties have been met by the creation of bargaining machinery in the form of Wages Councils. Though originally established to deal with sweated trades in which wages were 'unduly low', the workers concerned were difficult to get into unions, some because they were scattered and immobile (such as women chain makers), and the others because they were alien immigrants fighting to obtain a footing for themselves in particular industries, such as boot and shoe finishing and furniture manufacture. But there were many other trades where trade unionism—and sometimes employers' associations—had little effective hold, so that from 1918 it has been explicitly the lack of adequate machinery for effective regulation of remuneration, as well as the amount of the wage, which has been the test of whether a Wages Council should be established.[1] Between 1918 and 1944, Councils were set up in such trades as baking, rubber manufacturing, fustian cutting and cutlery; since 1945, in the retail distribution of food, boots and shoes, tobacco and sweets, etc. The machinery created provided, as recommended by the Select Committee on *Home Work*, 1908,[2] for a board composed of equal numbers of representatives of employers and employees, and for an independent chairman and appointed members. But in its application to these trades this means that the workers' side consists of representatives of unions of which only a small fraction, 10 per cent or even 5 per cent, of the workers concerned are members, and that they bargain on behalf of the other

[1] There were difficulties in enforcing agreements on unorganized employers in the retail furnishing, bookselling and tobacco trades. The organizations on either side of the hairdressing trade were unrepresentative. The Rubber-Proofed Garment Wages Council was set up on application from both employers' and workers' organizations (Commission. Rep.; 1956 Non-Parl. Min. of Labour).

[2] Rep.; 1908 (246) viii.

90 or 95 per cent not members.[1] No doubt if the 'workers' side' can point to some substantial gains they claim to have obtained, they may be able to increase the membership, but the fundamental difficulties of union organization often remain[2] and many of the workers still think of the rise being given by 'the Government'. In principle, this situation is not different from that in which agreements have been independently negotiated in trades where unionism has been weak. And some of the practices of 'normal' collective bargaining have been adhered to, e.g. during the discussions the two sides may meet separately if need be.[3]

To meet the second difficulty, the enforceability of agreements, the Wages Councils' legislation has in effect taken a leaf out of the Report on *Industrial Agreements* intended to apply to more organized trades, expressing the view of the majority that agreements might be made binding on non-signatories, since the Councils' recommendations are embodied in Orders having statutory force.

This part of the machinery of collective bargaining has not been free from the difficulty which has beset the voluntary part, that of defining an 'industry' or 'trade', and this has been particularly true of the distributive trades. The grocery 'trade'—an early trouble—consists of the food branches of departmental stores, company chain stores, co-operative societies, local private chains, and small individual shops, and small mixed 'corner' shops; and an endeavour to represent all sections led at the outset to the establishment of a board of seventy-eight people.[4] The catering trades include luxury London hotels, chains of teashops, 'seasonal' Lake District and Scottish hotels, dockland sausage shops, unlicensed restaurants, industrial canteens, carmen's pull-ups—really a series of separate trades, each with a separate market as well as some competitive

[1] For a description of the methods of selecting each side's representatives on the early boards, see R. H. Tawney. *Minimum Rates in the Chainmaking Industry*. 1914. pp. 29–30; E. M. Burns. *Wages and the State*. 1926. pp. 192–3.

[2] In three cases, Tobacco, Rubber Reclamation and Chain Making, organization on both sides has now advanced and the Councils have been dissolved.

[3] For a description of the procedure see C. W. Guillebaud, *The Wages Council System in Great Britain*. 1958. pp. 16–21.

[4] For the definition of the four retail food trades, see *Retail Food Trades*. Com. Rep. App. I; 1947 Non-Parl. Min. of Labour & National Service. On the size of the grocery trade board, see E. M. Burns. op. cit. p. 91.

overlap with its neighbouring catering trade and employing different
kinds of labour. The attempts to grapple with this problem in 1926,
1930 and 1931 and the work of the Catering Wages Commission
since 1943 in sorting out manageably separate trades has still left
some residual problems. Then the recommendation that drivers of
vans, who move freely from one retail trade to another, should be
covered by the Wages Council for the trade for which they work
and should not, as suggested by the T.G.W.U., be dealt with
together as transport workers, contrasts with the decision that hair-
dressers in hotels should be covered by the Hairdressing Wages
Council because they pass to and from other hairdressing establishments. Other difficulties included those of dealing with such intermingled trades as those of books, stationery, tobacco and sweets.

7. FAILURE TO AGREE: EMERGENCY BARGAINING MACHINERY

What if the unions and the employers fail to reach an agreement?
If the use of the industry's own machinery for dealing with disputes
does not produce a settlement?[1] The alternative to a strike or lock-
out is the use of emergency processes requiring outside aid, and the
terms 'failure to agree', to 'report a dispute', to 'report an issue'
denote important steps, after the normal processes of bargaining
have been exhausted. For in the British view it is essential to the
success of voluntary collective bargaining that the parties should
rely as completely as possible on their own powers of negotiation
and that neither should look to state intervention until every stage
in the procedure provided by the agreements has been gone through
and an impasse reached. That is to say, nothing should be done to

[1] In the inter-war years, during a number of disputes in nation-wide key
industries whose repercussions seriously affected or threatened employment
in other industries, the T.U.C. General Council set up Mediation Committees
which, as the name suggests, acted as mediators between the union and the
employer concerned, or the union and the Government, meeting the union
and employer or Government separately, or accompanying the union to the
meetings. There is no doubt that these good offices were often of great assistance in 'bridging gaps' and promoting settlements, and that its members
gained a great deal of experience in the timing and conduct of this work.
T.U.C. Rule No. 11 expressly gives to the General Council the right, in circumstances of this kind, to intervene either on request or on its own initiative.
Clause 11 (b) makes it quite clear that these powers are not to be exercised
as long as there is a prospect of the difference being amicably settled by the
trade's own machinery of negotiation.

interfere with, replace or undermine voluntary negotiating arrangements.[1]

The arrangements for 'arbitration' may take the form of a Court, which makes an *award*, or a Court of Inquiry, which may make a *recommendation*. For reference to the Industrial Court, the consent of both parties is necessary, for reference to a Court of Inquiry, of neither. The awards of the Industrial Court are not legally enforceable, but it is held that if accepted or acted upon they may form a term or condition of the contract of employment. The Court of Inquiry makes recommendations only. It is in line with our traditional policy that none of these bodies can be set to work unless the arrangements agreed between the parties have failed to produce a settlement. Certain Acts relating to particular industries, e.g. the Sugar Industry Act, and the Road Haulage Wages Act, 1938, as well as many voluntarily negotiated collective agreements, provide that if there is *failure to agree* the dispute shall go to the Industrial Court; and often both unions and employers may undertake to accept the Court's award as binding. The prohibition of strikes during World War II deprived unions of their final weapon, and in return there was established a National Arbitration Tribunal, to which either party could 'report' a dispute, and all employers, whether members of associations or not, had to observe the terms and conditions as settled by bodies of workpeople and employers which had a substantial proportion of workers and employers as members. When after the war prohibition on strikes was lifted, the Tribunal was reconstituted as the Industrial Disputes Tribunal, the requirement that employers must observe recognized terms was replaced by provisions giving unions the power not only to 'report' a *dispute*, but to 'report' an *issue* as to whether an individual employer should observe recognized terms and conditions.[2] The unions could thus obtain a decision where a reference could not be jointly agreed by both sides, the issues procedure was a suitable means of enforcing widely agreed conditions on non-federated or minority employers, and the unions had an

[1] Mr. Turner has pointed out that in the seven years 1945 to 1951, 70 per cent of the aggregate amount of increases in wage rates was secured by voluntary negotiations, 17 per cent through statutory wage-fixing bodies, 5 per cent by sliding scales and the remaining 8 per cent by arbitration. H. A. Turner. *Arbitration—a Study of Industrial Experience.* [1952.] p. 28.

[2] *Industrial Disputes Order 1951.* Article 10; S.I. 1951, no. 1376.

opportunity to seek redress in some sections of employment, particularly of non-manual workers, where unions were often not recognized and the strike weapon was or could not be used. The Order also contained restrictions designed to prevent a breakaway union or unorganized group from going to the Tribunal and up-setting a wage agreement accepted by the union. Some of these advantages were lost when this experiment in compulsory arbitration came to an end because the employers and unions could not agree as to the conditions in which arbitration should be compulsory; the Government then decided to rely on the extension of voluntary bargaining and allowed the order to lapse in 1959. *The Terms and Conditions of Employment Act*, 1959, Section 8, however, replaced the 'issue' procedure by one which enabled the employers' associa-tions or unions who were parties to an agreement, and who repre-sented a substantial proportion of employers and workers, to ask that a '*claim*' that an employer was not following recognized terms and conditions should be referred to the Industrial Court. If satisfied with the claim, the Court could make an award requiring an employer to observe them, which would be legally enforceable as an implied term of the contract of employment. Some non-manual workers' unions, however, which were struggling to secure 'recog-nition', were excluded from access to arbitration by the require-ment that its union must represent a substantial proportion of the workers concerned.[1] The Court of Inquiry has a different purpose. The parties may be unwilling to go to the Industrial Court or be unlikely to accept its award; if other means of producing a settlement fail, the Minister may refer the matter to a Court of Inquiry, in order that Parliament and the public may be informed of the facts of the dispute. If it wishes, that Court may make recommendations to which public opinion may be expected to give due weight, but no one is bound to accept them. For obvious reasons, the power to set up such a Court is used sparingly, and only in matters of public importance.

The effectiveness of arrangements for arbitration naturally depends in the last resort on the general attitude of those concerned: some matters of dispute, e.g. an encroachment on existing wage standards or on the functions of management, may be resisted with vigour and passion, and a trial of strength by strike or lock-out

[1] T.U.C., Blackpool, 1957. Rep. pp. 339–41.

may be preferred to an unfavourable decision by an arbitrator; or the history of industrial relations in the firm or industry may be one either of embitterment or of mutual accommodation. If it became the practice not to accept the awards of the Industrial Court, proceedings before it would be reduced to a stage in industrial negotiation, and its effectiveness as an agency of industrial peace greatly weakened.

The general mood on arbitration varies and there may be waves of disinclination to accept it. Such a wave occurred in 1955–62. Faced with periodic inflationary pressures together with more vigorous union policies, in the pursuit of stable prices the Government swung between attempts to restrain the rise of wages and salaries by such measures as enunciating for public services the principle that pay increases should be offset by compensating economies, overruling a Whitley Council award to National Health Service employees, imposing a wages pause for three months in certain public employments, referring back or postponing the operation of Wages Council Awards, not approving an award made to civil servants by agreed machinery, and on the other hand trying to prevent interruptions of employment through large-scale strikes on the railways by subsidizing the Transport Commission and by discouraging the engineering and port employers from resisting pay claims. In consequence, the unions became more chary in their attitude to arbitration: in 1959 the Printing Unions declined action by the Ministry of Labour and accepted the offices, on an informal basis, of an independent person, Lord Birkett.

What are the matters which can usefully be referred to the Court or Tribunal? First, wages disputes. Here it is necessary to bear in mind what it is they are called upon to decide. It is not whether the whole basis of the wages and salary structure of the country should be altered, whether town clerks should be paid more than road-menders or road-menders more than town clerks, whether the school caretaker should be paid as much as the headmaster or station staff as much as the railways' chief accountant, the labourer as much as the foreman. The dispute comes before them as a dispute about wages, expressed usually in a difference between two figures, the union's and the employer's, and that difference, large or small, is simply a variation in existing rates of pay. It is this they have to adjudicate upon. Sometimes, it is true, over a period of time a succession of awards may move an industry higher up the scale as compared with like industries, but then it is almost always both a step by step change, and a recognition of an alteration in the demand for and supply of the class of labour involved as a result of broad economic movements. Whatever part may be played by the bargaining between miners and the Coal Board, the miners' pay would have improved anyway. The arguments of each side and any reasoning of the Court or Tribunal as to where the balance between the two figures should be struck, and any economic theory they involve, have to be read in the context of a dispute about the size of a variation of an existing rate. Of these more will be said later; here we are concerned with the procedure only as a means of overcoming a 'failure to agree' without resort to a strike or lock-out. And this means that the task of the Court or Tribunal is not one simply of finding the 'economically right' rate or the one which causes least unemployment, but also a rate acceptable to both parties. If the preliminary bargaining processes which have failed have, nevertheless, reduced the margin to a residual difference, though both parties may be 'obstinate' about it, the purely quantitative task of the Court or Tribunal is easier; but if it is large, the problem is more difficult, because the difference between award and claim may still be regarded by one side or both as substantial enough to be worth a trial of strength.

Secondly, there are questions of principle. These may concern, on the union side, some vital method by which a union fortifies the wage rate, such as the allocation of workmen to machines, the number of apprentices, the right to be consulted on a piece-work system, or the right to elect a shop steward; on the employers' side, some essential function of management. These are amongst the hardest for an arbitrator to deal with, and neither party may be very willing to submit them. Even pointing out how these questions are dealt with in other firms and industries does not always produce conviction.

Thirdly, there is a sharp distinction between interpreting an old agreement and making a new one. The former can be a good field for arbitration, for a new case not foreseen at the time of signature of the agreement may arise, and the question is simply one of extending to it the scope and intention of the agreement. But the fundamental assumptions on which an agreement was based may alter: there may be a change in the conditions of trade, in foreign competition, in technique or in prices. And these may suggest a substantial change in wages or the incorporation of new principles into the agreement. These questions involve elements of forecast and of opinion quite different from the extension or adaptation of a clause in an existing agreement to a new case.

Finally, its awards show that the Court will take cognizance of the code and conventions of collective bargaining to which reference has already been made on pp. 26–9. It will be seen that they have noted not only breaches of the procedure agreed between the workers and the employers, but have given support to the understandings, and have reinforced the moral obligations of the parties. Not the least of its services has been its steady insistence that the parties put themselves in the wrong if they break the code.

What these principles mean in operation is best understood by looking at the awards themselves. In each of the six years from 1951 to 1957 the Industrial Court made, on average, sixty-three awards. In the same period, the Industrial Disputes Tribunal dealt with an average of 150 cases, most of them minor ones concerning the interpretation of agreements, formal or even informal, or their application to new types of cases; and there is no doubt that this piece of machinery has provided a simple and effective means for preventing them from being a continued source of friction or growing into more serious disputes. The following are examples:

On wages and conditions: Claims to increase of wages of roadmen, established; of building trade workers, not established (Industrial Disputes Tribunal, Nos. 343, 385, 1953). Claims of radio operators on fishing vessels, in part established, in part not established (Industrial Court, No. 2457, 1953); upgrading of a local authority for wage purposes (Industrial Disputes Tribunal, No. 442, 1953); wages of certain road transport workers not fair compared with those covered by Road Transport Wages Act (Industrial Court, Nos. 2221, 1949; 2443, 1953); award in favour of employers that workers should operate a modified costing system (Industrial Disputes Tribunal, No. 355, 1953); award in favour of union that the company should complete an incentive scheme (National Arbitration Tribunal, No. 1459, 1950); absence of any production incentive (National Arbitration Tribunal, No. 1182, 1948); award in favour of union which asked for replacement of small group piece rates by a single group piece rate (Industrial Court, No. 2472,

1953). Claim for further holidays with pay not established (National Arbitration Tribunal, No. 1561, 1950). Dismissal of a worker justified (Industrial Court, No. 2223, 1949; National Arbitration Tribunal, No. 1489, 1950). Employers held not to be violating House of Commons Fair Wages Resolution, 1946, or preventing men from being trade unionists (Industrial Court, No. 2481, 1953).

On the revision or interpretation of agreements: No alteration of circumstances had occurred to justify employers terminating an agreement (Industrial Court, No. 2475, 1953); a union's interpretation of an agreement that they were at liberty to approach individual employers to secure more favourable terms than those agreed was confirmed (Industrial Court, No. 2431, 1953).

On methods of negotiation: Joint machinery for maintenance of discipline and elimination of absenteeism should be considered (Industrial Court, No. 2274, 1950); in a wage difference where two unions were involved, the Colliery Winders and National Union of Mineworkers, the two unions should negotiate to settle their differences (National Arbitration Tribunal, No. 1541, 1950).

Some of the awards on wages have set out the economic or other principles upon which the Court based its decision: these are analysed at a later stage.

The working of these semi-judicial processes by no means eliminates all bargaining, for what they are concerned with is not the interpretation of a legal commercial contract, but the terms on which the many persons represented by the two negotiating sides should agree to enter into a contract of employment. The effective use of them in a major dispute may therefore require skilful management on the part of the Minister of Labour as well as of the two parties. For the Minister may not set the Industrial Court in motion without the consent of both of them, and one or possibly both may be unwilling. Experience since 1945 has shown that the unions may be unwilling because recent awards in other and parallel disputes have given the unions concerned less than they are themselves determined to get if they can; and there are examples of unions who have refused arbitration by the Court, rejected recommendations by the Court of Inquiry and have yet obtained more by direct negotiation and through conciliation by the Minister of Labour. Employers may be reluctant also, because they fear that the Court may merely 'split the difference'. If they dislike this prospect strongly enough and anticipate that pressure will make acceptance of reference to

the Court unavoidable, they may decline to make an offer to the
unions on the ground that it will be better to present the Court with
the choice between splitting the difference between, say, 15s. and
nothing than between 15s. and 5s. At these delicate stages the
Minister may also have difficulties. If both sides refuse to go to
the Industrial Court, the next step may, but need not be, a Court
of Inquiry. A Court must hear both sides, consider and report,
and this may take time, and in the meantime strike notices may be
expiring. The Minister may therefore press both sides to make
concessions enough to enable them to meet again to negotiate on
the remaining differences. These residual differences may not be
'money', but whether, as in a recent case, there should be a wage
increase on condition that there is a standstill for a year and that
restrictive practices should cease, etc., or a smaller increase free of
conditions. Some Courts have therefore been set up in the hope of
preventing a strike, others in order to end one. In the swings
between inflation and attempts at stabilization which the last decade
has witnessed, the Minister could scarcely do other than bear in
mind not only the technique of handling these delicate situations,
but also the need to avoid both industrial disputes and wage-induced
inflation; his course of action must in some degree be influenced by
which of these two evils he regards as the worse at the time.

8. STRIKES: BREAKDOWN OF NEGOTIATIONS OR WEAPON?

The place in collective bargaining to be accorded to strikes
depends a great deal on the point of view. Are they weapons of
last resort, turned to only if all other methods have failed? or have
they a place in the armory, for use alongside or instead of other
methods, according to circumstances? or are they inevitable inci-
dents in the class struggle against capitalism, desirable even if
technically 'lost', because they emphasize the class struggle and
give the workers the experience and discipline needed for the over-
throw of capitalism? All three opinions have existed side by side
amongst British trade unionists, the degree of support accorded to
each depending on the mood and circumstances of the time. The
latter, more radical view was freely expressed by some sections of
trade unionists during 1917–20, for example, but was also held by
some much earlier in the nineteenth century. That Lenin should
hold it was understandable enough, not only because it is the

D

Marxist view, but also because Russian industry was then owned and controlled largely by the State and by foreign capital, there was no real outlet through political democracy, and the unions were bound to think of broad social and political objectives; collective bargaining did not therefore occupy the central position in Russian as it did in British and American trade unionism. In Britain it has not been widely enough held to produce many strikes deeply imbued with those motives. Rather the swings of emphasis have been between the first two notions, and when inclined to the more belligerent of the two, these have shown themselves rather as a greater readiness to take offence, to 'down tools', to be uncompromising on a larger range of the less important matters, and to impatience with and disregard of long and protracted negotiations: strikes are more numerous, and sympathetic strikes more common. The way in which such a mood could develop and its influence on disputes was admirably analysed in the Commission of Inquiry's very intelligent study of the causes of industrial unrest in South Wales in 1917.[1] But even in troubled times most strikes are in the main about specific industrial issues, and the left-wing belligerent pursuing an 'anti-capitalism' policy knows that men cannot be brought out unless this is tied to a wage or similar issue. Strikes are therefore about wages and hours, the employment of non-unionists, dismissals, victimization, recognition, and 'sympathetic' strikes about matters which unions feel vital to unionism generally, such as miners' wages and the technique of bargaining in 1926, or the 'open shop', as in the Thomson dispute of 1953.

There is much that is interesting in the technique and management of strikes. They may affect few or many, be local, district or national; may be formally declared at the end of a long series of negotiations, or be 'lightning' strikes. Men may engage in a 'stay-out', a 'stay-in' or 'sit-down' strike to enforce their view in a work-shop dispute. There may be a 'token' strike as a protest;[2] indeed, some had urged that in 1926 a 'token' general strike would have been better than the form actually adopted. Now, when inflation

[1] *Industrial Unrest*. Com. Rep. No. 7; 1917–18 Cd. 8668, xv. See P. and G. Ford. *Breviate of Parliamentary Papers, 1917–1939.* 1951. pp. 317–18.

[2] For example, in the 1957 engineering dispute, see *Engineering and Allied Employers' National Federation and . . . Confederation of Shipbuilding and Engineering Unions. Dispute.* Ct. of Inquiry. Rep. paras. 24, 26; 1956–57 Cmnd. 159, xiv.

has meant high wages, while union subscriptions and dispute pay have remained stationary or have not proportionately increased, and financing a long dispute is more difficult, there have been experiments with 'staggered' strikes and with 'guerrilla' strikes,[1] i.e. short strikes at selected sites only, perhaps in rotation. The strike or threat of a strike of electrical and other workers engaged in preparing for a trade exhibition or festival a few days before the publicly-announced opening has become so common a practice that one must presume that by now it must be normally allowed for in estimating. While these variations in the technique of in-fighting obviously have some bearing on the speed and cost of securing an acceptance of a claim, the pressure which can be exerted by strikes varies between industries and processes. A strike of laundry workers might not greatly inconvenience the private householder, since there is obviously more than one way of mitigating its effects, though hotels, etc., might soon be in real difficulties. But a great transport strike may soon add to the inconvenience to the travelling public a dislocation of industrial freight and industrial idleness. A strike of workers on some key process may soon bring other processes to a stop; of this recent examples are internal transport workers, maintenance engineers, workers on castings; the stoppage of skilled men has meant that unskilled men, members of a different union, have been stood off.

Unofficial strikes are those which are called contrary to the union rules by members, e.g. shop stewards, not authorized to call them. They have also sometimes been termed 'unconstitutional' in the limited sense that they may be in breach of procedure agreed with employers for settling disputes, but they may occur spontaneously because the collective agreement may be limited to wages and hours and not provide machinery for dealing with other difficulties, such as dismissals, because changes are made without consultation, or because it may take too long to wait for reference to Head Office. According to the T.U.C. inquiry, in about half the unofficial strikes the unions were at least sufficiently satisfied later to grant dispute pay, but in others, usually those against union policies or even the union itself, dispute pay was withheld.

Mr. Knowles' admirable study on *Strikes*[2] does all that can be done in the handling of strike statistics. If one takes a broad view

[1] Title, see n. 2, p. 40. Rep. para. 28; 1953–54 Cmd. 9084, xv.
[2] K. G. J. C. Knowles. *Strikes: A Study in Industrial Conflict.* 1952.

of strikes as a whole, these conclusions emerge. First, most strikes end in compromises; secondly, the compromises are often not just a splitting of the difference between two figures, but a mixture of diverse items—such as winning on a principle by giving up part of a rise, and may contain face-saving items for one or both sides. Thirdly, the gains in wages obtained after a strike are but a tiny proportion—say 1 per cent—of the gains obtained without a strike by negotiation or arbitration. Fourthly, in many disputes the unions must have obtained increases without striking simply because they possessed and could, if necessary, exercise the power to strike.

II

THE THEORY OF COLLECTIVE BARGAINING

1. The Unsuitability of Early Theories

IF economics is 'a method, a technique of analysis rather than a doctrine', then we have to ask what parts of economic theory it is best to use in this problem. We can at once dispense with the repetitive task of reviewing theories held in the earlier part of the nineteenth century for, as Cannan observed,[1] they were not well adapted to deal with the problem of trade unionism. The facts to be explained and the problems in which the economists were then really interested were different from those of to-day. In general, in the world of their day, the wage bargains were between individual workmen and individual employers, though, as Adam Smith observed, there were sometimes tacit agreements amongst employers, and John Gast's evidence before the Committee on the *Combination Laws*, 1825,[2] showed the working of somewhat primitive forms of union organization in some of the older crafts. Despite a famous effort by Adam Smith, they were less interested in the relative wage rates of different occupations than in the division of the total product between wages and the other categories of income, and their discussion was really in terms of a single wage rate, the 'general level' of wages, Ricardo treating the wages of different kinds of skill as multiples of so much normal labour. Since, in any case, they regarded the stock of wage capital as fixed, so that one group of workers could obtain a rise in wages only at the expense of other groups, there was no room for a theory of collective bargaining. And the wage fund theory presently faded out through its own inadequacy.

Similarly, the bitter hostility with which attempts at trade union activity were regarded by employers and the propertied classes, who feared the consequences to their own economic position and perhaps the loss of power to exercise petty tyrannies, placed trade unions in

[1] E. Cannan. *Theories of Production and Distribution*. 3rd ed. 1922. pp. 392–5.

[2] Sel. Cttee. Mins. of ev. pp. 298–318; 1825 (417) iv.

43

a position of requiring an ethical defence: they were justified because they were needed to put the bargaining strength of the propertyless worker, 'unable to wait', more on a level with that of the employer. Doctrines of 'bargaining strength' in this general sense,[1] economic in form but ethical in purport, served an historic purpose in that they helped to remove or soften the disapproval of trade unions and created an easier atmosphere[2] in which wage bargains could be negotiated with them and their legal position regulated. But they do not, however, throw much light on how much collective bargaining can accomplish, especially in a world in which all but 10 per cent of the workers are either 'unionized' or have their wages regulated by statutory bodies, in conditions of nearly full, full or over-full employment.

In the next phase matters were carried further: it was established that the employers' demand curve for labour was based on its net product. Any movement above or below the equilibrium wage (marginal net product) would lead either to unemployment or to labour shortages which would press back the wage to its equilibrium level. While this theory was more liberal and optimistic in tone, since wages could be raised by a shift of the curve of net product through increased efficiency, many writers confined themselves to or emphasized the general conclusion that there was still an upper limit beyond which unions could not raise wages except by restricting the entry of competing workers, either overtly through apprenticeship or other restrictive rules, or directly and simply by setting a high standard rate of wages at which some workers would not be employed.

2. IS A TRADE UNION A LABOUR 'TRUST'? SHOULD MONOPOLY THEORY BE APPLIED?

Whereas the correction of any deviation from the equilibrium wage depended on the strength of competition between employers seeking labour on one side and between workers seeking employment on the other, in the contemporary labour market wages in

---

[1] For example, Adam Smith. *Wealth of Nations.* Bk. I, chap. VIII. For an interesting critical examination of theories of labour's disadvantage, see W. H. Hutt. *The Theory of Collective Bargaining.* 1930. pp. 1–48.

[2] It was reported to the author by one of the men's representatives of the 'Firemen's Movement', H. Charleton, later M.P. for Leeds South, that at a meeting in 1904 with a railway company's representatives, they were not offered seats, but kept standing.

different industries are settled by separately negotiated collective bargains between a trade union trying to act as a 'single seller' of labour and an employers' association trying to act as a 'single buyer' of labour. Should we then apply the theory of monopoly? Is a trade union, especially one which has obtained exclusive bargaining rights, a labour trust? Unions have for long been denounced as monopolies, and in external appearance they appear so, since they endeavour to eliminate competition between the members. But a union does not itself produce or sell the commodity it controls, labour, nor receive payment for it. It could, indeed, itself try to undertake contracts, as the Builders' Guild did in 1833[1] under Owen's influence and in 1920 in the experiments associated with the name of Malcolm Sparkes; or theoretically, it could contract as a union to supply the requisite labour to an employer supplying the materials and undertaking the responsibility for and risks of the contract. But it does none of these things: it could be more fitly described as a 'labour cartel' fixing the wages and other conditions on which its individual members are permitted to sell their services to the individual employers. But it cannot destroy men in order to maintain their value, as monopolies have sometimes destroyed surplus stocks. It does not reduce the price of labour as the amount supplied increases, but tries to get the standard wage for every workman. It could certainly try, as a monopoly may, to obtain maximum net revenue, e.g. the maximum aggregate total sum of wages, but since that might lead to unemployment, it could make its aim the maximum amount of work at the standard rate. Then while many monopolies face unorganized consumers, in Britain to-day a trade union in the great industries has to bargain with organized employers. Consideration such as these led MacGregor (1906) and Wieser (1914)[2] to conclude that if unions were monopolies, they were a weak variety.

3. UNIONS AND THEIR BARGAINING STRENGTH

What constitutes the measure of 'strength' of a trade union or 'labour cartel' as a bargaining unit? A parallel question for a combination of manufacturers would be, what proportion of the

[1] R. W. Postgate. *The Builders' History.* 1923. Chaps. 4 and 5.
[2] D. H. MacGregor. *Industrial Combination.* 1906. Pt. II. Chap. III. F. von Wieser. *Social Economy.* Translated by A. F. Hinrichs. 1927. pp. 375–8.

output must it control in order to be able to set the price? In many cases it has been substantially less than 100 per cent. The residue of output may come from a number of small, independent firms willing to accept the lead of the major firms or fearful of what would happen if the organized group turned its competitive powers against them and deliberately undersold them. A union is unlikely to try to undersell non-unionists! The demands for a closed shop, refusal to work with non-unionists and the pressure of social opinion in the neighbourhood are its weapons. Various guesses, derived empirically from trials of strength, have been made of the proportion of any group of workers which a union must enrol to be able to set the rate: e.g. 75 per cent. But a proportion sufficient to enable the union to negotiate satisfactorily could be disastrously small in the event of a strike in which unenrolled members continued to work—a situation which could arise if the workers in some areas were organized and in others not. With the cessation of war production after World War I, followed by the trade depression, the general and women's unions suffered great losses of membership, but were able to continue to negotiate effectively for a long time on the strength of the prestige they had acquired at the peak of their membership, both because the employers did not know their numerical strength, and because it was often convenient to continue to negotiate rates applicable to every firm. A general union has often by its prestige negotiated new rates in factories or other work places in which it had no or few members, hoping to get new members as the result of it; and a success in one factory where there are members may make it possible to obtain increases in another factory in the same area where there are few or none. A fear of or a desire for security from a strike, perhaps the feeling that there may be a long run gain in paying a standard rate which other employers will not fall below, may influence employers to accept this situation. And, of course, they do not necessarily know how many of their workers are in the union, and are not able to contest a union organizer's discreetly worded claim to represent the employees. On the other hand, there is clearly some percentage of enrolment which is insufficient. Thus, the committees set up under the Wages Councils Act to advise whether such councils should be set up in the retail trades found that in the food trades, hairdressing, drapers', outfitters' and footwear trades not more than 10 per cent of the employees were members; in the wholesale and retail bread and confectionery trades not more than 15 per cent (two-thirds of whom were co-operative employees); whilst amongst booksellers, newsagents, tobacconists, etc., union membership was uneven, small or negligible. The inability of workers to obtain adequate wages on account of this weakness was one ground for recommending the establishment of wages councils.

The 'strength' of unions in this sense is not always easy to assess. In 1960 there were 16,047,000 males and 8,417,000 females employed: and there were 7,860,000 males and 1,943,000 females in trade unions. The small proportion of women in trade unions is due mainly to weakness in what are, from the union point of view, 'desert areas'—shop assistants, the typing and clerical staffs in many offices and private domestic workers. The gap between the two figures for men is due to the fact that many in the upper administrative and executive trades are not gathered into unions, nor are considerable numbers in various trades in smaller towns and villages. But the 'strength' of unions, i.e. the proportions of workers in the various industries and occupations who are members, is not always easy to state, because the union boundaries do not correspond to the boundaries of the industries or occupations as defined in the available statistical sources. We know that in coal mining, railway transport and port work, for example, there is substantially complete unionization; but craft unions may have a membership in many different industries, the kind of skill for which they cater may not correspond to any census or Ministry of Labour definition, so that we do not know the precise size of the 'constituency' from which they have to recruit. Then, though there may be a high proportion of workmen in the unions, those members may be shared between two unions which have different industrial policies, as railway drivers and firemen are between the A.S.L.E.F. and the N.U.R. Or the membership may be unstable. Thus the great T.G.W.U., with a membership of 1,318,000, had in its ranks not only highly stable groups of better-paid men—busmen, dock workers, road transport men, etc.—but a large floating membership of 'ins and outs', mostly general labourers, of about a third of the total: in one year about one-third of the membership lapsed and one-third were 'new members'.[1] Again, though a large proportion of seafarers are members of the National Union of Seamen, they do not work on shore in a factory for a weekly wage, but are away

[1] J. Goldstein, *The Government of British Trade Unions*. 1952.

at sea for longer or shorter periods; and the difficulties of organizing them in the early stages is vividly brought out by J. Havelock Wilson, General Secretary of the N.U.S., in his autobiography, *My Stormy Voyage through Life* (1925).

While, therefore, some unions have effective bargaining powers because they include all or a large proportion of the workers in the industry or occupation, and others have limited powers because they are 'weak', others, such as the T.G.W.U., are able successfully to negotiate agreements covering even the unstable elements of the membership. The strongly organized stable groups it also includes afford moral support to the less stable; and the prestige it derives from the publicized agreements made on behalf of busmen, dockers, etc., makes it easier to secure agreements for general labourers without strikes, even in those miscellaneous factories and sites where it has little support, or has no intention and probably could not call a successful strike for anything but a relatively short period. And when a big union of this kind deals with a large number of competing, relatively small employers, the union organizer may not only be a more experienced negotiator, but may also know more than the employer both about the labour market and about broader business trends.

4. FROM WHAT SOURCES CAN WAGE INCREASES BE OBTAINED?

One trade only

When we investigate the effect of a producer's or a trader's monopoly on output and price, we do so initially on the assumption that he will endeavour to maximize his gains, i.e. the difference between costs and the proceeds from sales. We know, of course, that while some monopolies have not been afraid to exert their full powers in this way, others have been more restrained: they have feared that if they did so there might be a public outcry and interference by the legislature,[1] or that high prices and profits might tempt new firms into the market, for security of gains as well as maximum gains enter into their calculations. Occasionally some great concern has contended that it has not exercised its full strength in driving out independent small competitors because it 'believed in

[1] For example, *Distribution and Prices of Agricultural Produce*. Dept. Cttee. Interim Rep.; *Milk and Milk Products*. pp. 45-6, 85; 1923 Cmd. 1854, ix. (Reprinted 1924 Non-Parl.)

a certain amount of competition', although it could be shown that in some circumstances at least the monopoly had done its worst and was not able to prevent their survival.[1] Despite this variety of circumstances limiting the full operation of the maximization principle, the use of the assumption is justified because unless a business operated in this sort of way, it may well not survive. If, then, we think of trade unions as 'labour cartels', can we make a similar assumption? But since a union does not buy or sell, or receive any proceeds, there is no 'total sum' of which it has direct knowledge. What, then, does it 'maximize'? Does it set out to 'maximize' anything at all? Could it maximize the total aggregate sum received in wages by those of its numbers covered by the agreement? But a rise of wages which gave this result could also cause some unemployment. A trust can maximize its gains by restricting its output, but it then need not buy as much material or use as much labour as before: those effects and losses fall on others. Some of the unemployment, on the other hand, would fall on the union's own members. We have, therefore, to look at the possible choices which may confront a union, the way they present themselves and what affects them.

There are thus two ways of approaching the problem. An economist is interested in the interdependence of the various parts of the economic order, in the chain of reactions by which a price rise, say, of a particular kind of labour, has its effects carried into other parts of the system. But the propositions setting out these possibilities give the system an appearance of rigidity it does not possess: in fact, it has a good deal of flexibility. And a union which paid too much regard to distant consequences would soon end in doing nothing at all. Like a business, it has to ignore the more remote repercussions of its actions, which may, anyhow, be lost in the cross-currents of the business world. We may also, therefore, put ourselves in the position of a union leader, and survey the economic scene to see where and what are the sources from which increases of wages can be obtained.

Suggestions as to what these might be can be gathered from the speeches of leaders and the statements of claim and evidence presented from time to time at inquiries into wage claims and disputes. Few inquiries range over the whole field of possibilities,

[1] E. A. G. Robinson. *Monopoly*. 1941. p. 32.

but looked at as a whole, the suggestions are that wages could be increased in three ways: by raising the price of labour, by raising the price of the product and by enlarging the resources from which an increase can be paid, either by improving a firm's or an industry's technological efficiency, or its efficiency as a buying and selling business unit. The first of these usually attracts most attention. But it involves two quite distinct questions: (a) in what circumstances can a union raise wages; and (a narrower and more searching one) (b) since a rise in price checks demand, in what circumstances can a union raise wages without creating some unemployment? We shall deal with the former question first.

Wage claims can be brought up for discussion in a number of different forms. A craft or a clerical union may make a claim for its members in a given industry without any particular reference to or discussion with any other grades of workers, an industrial union or federation with exclusive bargaining rights may present one for all grades simultaneously, or separate unions representing different grades may each simultaneously make a claim for their respective members. In the first case the effect on unit costs might be small, and the problem which emerges be one rather of differentials within the industry. An industrial union's claim for all grades would affect both unit cost and the relative levels and attractiveness of the industry as a whole compared with others, but part at least of the problem of differentials would have been put out of the way, because the grades or crafts within the industrial union or federation must have already agreed on the relationship of the wages for each grade. But when separate unions present simultaneous claims the problems both of differentials within the industry and of the wages in the industry as a whole compared with others may have to be considered. In 1951, for example, the three railway unions presented simultaneously requests for an increase of 10 per cent for N.U.R. men, 7½ per cent for railway clerks and 15 per cent for loco men.[1] Both the loco men and clerks disliked increases for the lower grades only, and the Court agreed that wages in mining and agriculture had risen more than in the railway service, but argued that these industries were undermanned and it was national policy to raise their position. Unless distinctions such as these are borne in mind,

[1] *Applications for an Improvement in Wages and Salaries made ... by the N.U.R., the A.S.L.E.F., and the Railway Clerks' Assoc.* Ct. of Inquiry. Rep. pp. 36, 40, 51; 1950–51 Cmd. 8154, xvi.

no satisfactory answer about the possible sources of wage increases can be given.

Marshall's example, which provides a convenient starting point, is a claim of the first type, that of a trade union of one craft, plasterers, operating in a single industry against competing employers. It was a kind of case common when he wrote and common even just after World War I, when a considerable number of industries were brought within the field of trade unionism. Marshall had not witnessed the great endeavour made, in order to ensure the success of large housing programmes after both World Wars, to increase the building industry's manpower by raising wages. With such an increase of demand and shortages of particular kinds of labour, wages would obviously have risen in free competition without the aid of the unions: to get an idea of the sources of wage increases over and above this it is best to think first, as Marshall does, of the plasterer's claim in stable conditions of trade. Plasterers do not work in isolation, but alongside the men of other crafts and with other factors of production, to produce a final product, houses. What limits are set to any rise of pay through its repercussions on these co-operant factors? From what source is the pay rise to come? From economies on plastering work? from reductions in the pay of the other crafts or of capital? from the consumers through a rise in the price of houses? The propositions which Marshall advances may be summarized briefly: the results will depend on (i) the elasticity of demand for plasterers' work; (ii) the elasticity of supply of the other co-operating factors, and (iii) the elasticity of demand for houses and other buildings.

(i) *Raising the price of labour*

What, then, is the scope for increasing the contents of the pay packet? To begin with the first of these conditions, the answer depends on whether by a rise in wages we mean a rise of pay per man or increased total earnings of all the workers. For the rise may restrict the volume of employment, and if it does, then a rise in pay per man of those still employed might be accompanied by a rise or a fall in the total earnings of the whole group of workers, according to the proportion put off work. Naturally, if the demand were increasing, no one might be unemployed and more workers might be engaged, but that is not our problem.

But if demand were stable, a given percentage rise in wages (to a level above marginal net product) would lead to a fall in the demand for that kind of labour; if the demand were inelastic, there would be a smaller percentage fall of demand, a rise in the aggregate amount of wages received by the workers still in employment and some unemployment of men unable to get work at the new rate. In terms of aggregate proceeds the workers as a whole would have gained, and if the union had been in the habit of itself selling the labour in bulk and distributing the total received amongst all its members on a pre-arranged principle, all the individual workers would have gained something. But it is individuals, not unions, who make contracts of employment, so that those in work would be better off, and those out of work would be without wages. If, on the other hand, the demand for the labour concerned were elastic, the rise in price of labour would be followed by a greater percentage fall in the demand for it, a smaller aggregate amount of wages would be received by the group, and while those still employed would be better off, a greater amount of unemployment would be caused than if demand were inelastic. Thus, maximizing the gains for those remaining in employment might or might not maximize them for the group of workers as a whole. The one circumstance in which both the group of workers as a whole and each individual would gain would be when the demand for that type of labour was completely inelastic.

These propositions merely indicate the relationships which have to be investigated: what happens will depend on what the elasticities of supply and demand are in fact. Thus when the cost of one component or process, such as plastering, is a small percentage of the total cost of the final product, a modest rise in its price will have such a small effect on the total cost of the product that the demand for it and therefore for that kind of labour will be little affected. This condition of inelasticity of demand for each of the several components or processes used in house-building—of which stoves and grates, drains, etc., are other examples—explains why it was easy for monopolistic 'rings round the house' each to manipulate and control prices on the scale shown in the report of the Committee on *Trusts*, 1919.[1] But the *combined* effect of a 10 per cent rise in the price of only those materials fully controlled by price agreements was estimated to increase the cost of 300,000 £250 cottages by £1,095,000. The numerous crafts in the building industry are in an

[1] Rep. pp. 36–7; 1918 Cd. 9236, xiii.

analogous position, each of them accounting for but a small part of the total cost of a house, so that any one of them alone is in a favourable position for bargaining. But when eighteen unions concerned in the building industry act together—in order to keep the pay of men working alongside one another in line, and because 'union is strength'—their aggregate wages are then a substantial part of the total cost, and if all get a rise, the effect on the price of and demand for house room is more substantial. Shipyard unions in the Confederation are clearly in the same position. Again, there may be some inelasticity when there is a wide spread between manufacturer's cost and retail price. The fact that the cost of women's labour in the making of some women's garments was but a small part of final price to the consumer, no doubt helped to make it easier for the Trade Board to raise the pay of these sweated workers, without proportionately increasing the price to the consumers. But in coal mining, labour costs are a large proportion of total costs, a circumstance which helps to explain the great strikes and lock-outs of the inter-war years. For coal-owners were naturally as disposed to resist increases of wages as they were to turn to them as the one possible source of substantial reductions of cost when trade was bad. By contrast, there is more room for a manoeuvre when a large part of costs are due to the use of an expensive material, such as cotton.

On the other hand, the elasticity of demand for labour also varies according to the extent to which a rise in its pay can be met by economizing in its use, by employing an alternative process, or by using machinery requiring few or less skilled workmen. Plastering work, for example, can be reduced by using plain brick or distempered walls, by substituting partitions in alternative materials such as glass and steel, etc. In a dispute between the London Master Printers and the London Typographical Society, the employers argued that the spread of miniature printing had led certain large customers, e.g. local authorities, to set up their own printing sections using machines operated by others than craftsmen.[1] The substitution of one kind of labour for another may be limited not only by technical possibilities, but also in some degree by employers' agreements with unions as to what kinds of workers should be

[1] *London Master Printers' Assoc., and the London Typographical Soc. and the Assoc. of the Correctors of the Press. Disputes.* Ct. of Inquiry. Rep. para. 34; 1955–56 Cmd. 9717, xxi.

employed on particular processes or which require consultation on the manning of new ones.

The effect on the volume of employment

When a union makes an agreement, it fixes wages and other conditions of work, but it does not, save in exceptional circumstances, fix the total numbers to be employed. While, therefore, there is a wide variety of circumstances in which a union can obtain a greater or lesser rise of wage per man, that rise may be quite consistent with either a fall or rise in the aggregate earnings of the whole group, according to whether many, few or no workers have lost employment because their labour has become too expensive, or more expensive than other means of doing the same job. We can leave aside for later consideration those cases of 'imperfect competition' in which a union can enforce a rise of pay without thereby diminishing the opportunities for their employment: there is clearly *some* rise of pay at which men will be put off work, and the processes by which this can occur need examination first. One objection sometimes raised can be put aside: it has been suggested that employers, especially in large works, cannot calculate the 'contribution' of any particular worker to the product and that therefore a rise of wages need not lead to the unemployment of 'marginal' workers. Though the conclusion may often be correct—we shall look at such cases later—the reason given for it is unacceptable. He can and does make some estimate: even in a large works, a departmental manager or foreman can tell him that this department is over-staffed, the other under-staffed, and he can transfer workers, or decide not to fill vacancies when they occur, as well as give notice. And unless it were possible to do this, both for workers and additions to capital, rational economic organization would be impossible, whether in private, nationalized or Soviet industry.

Misunderstanding is often caused by opposing employers and journalists who overplay their hand, and over-dramatize the effects of a wage rise, as if unemployment would forthwith ensue; though this sometimes happens, it is not often the case, because changes of this sort take place by slow adjustments at the margin which take some time to show themselves. But that these could be significant can be seen by the fact that if a man's working life in an industry were, say, forty years, then if recruitment ceased, the industry would fall to about half its size in twenty years—just the span of years between the two world wars and half a man's working life. The least predictable and least obvious, though often the real difficulty, is 'invisible unemployment'; i.e. the loss of the extra employment which an industry would have provided had labour unit costs been lower. The rank-and-file trade unionist might well be inclined to chuckle if an employer advanced such an argument: 'Are not all the members in full employment?' Yet the possibility is not unreal, for in a new industry growing in more than one country and competing in the international market, the relative levels of unit costs, including wage costs if they are an important item, would settle the relative size of the industry in each country. Too high a wage rate, like any other excessive cost, though it might leave the total volume of employment stable and thus seem satisfactory to the two bargaining parties, could lead to unemployment in the sense that growth would be arrested. The difficulty is that in such cases so many other factors may be operating, that it is not easy to establish what might be, until perhaps long after it has become history. When there are more vacancies than workers seeking them, men not employed in an industry on account of an 'excessive' wage rate can more easily find alternative jobs. This does not mean that the relative elasticities of demand and supply are without effect in the labour market (as distinct from being taken into account by the unions); on the contrary, they will determine the numbers of men not taken on in the industry, and this 'surplus' will then not be unemployed, but engaged in some other part of the field of employment. The 'unemployment' is then concealed in migration and diversion, and the effect of union policy is thus to redistribute labour between industries.

The choice in front of a union is, therefore, not always clear-cut. Unions have, indeed, been exhorted often enough to 'consider the unemployment' their insistence on a certain wage rate would cause, and to pursue as an objective maximum employment rather than maximum aggregate wages. If they have sometimes seemed deaf to these appeals, there have often been good grounds for it. For, in fact, the direct effect of a wage increase is by no means always predictable, nor the precise relationship of a wage rate and the level of unemployment always clear. Its influence may be obscured by the ups and downs of demand for the product, the progress of invention, etc. Nor would it always be practicable to accept the advice. In the inter-war years, before the present 'age of inflation',

E

they accepted reductions in bad times, though naturally trying to delay and ameliorate them, yet during a great trade collapse even severe wage cuts might not increase employment at all, because a proportion of the product is just not wanted. The amount of surplus capacity in the shipbuilding industry in 1930–34 was such that no tolerable wage cut would have kept open some of the shipyards bought up and dismantled by National Shipbuilders' Security Ltd. as redundant.[1] It would be possible to think of a condition of the labour market such that a union energetically seeking to maximize employment would logically find it part of the duty itself to propose a reduction of wage rates. But it would be unlikely to keep its members that way. Unions cannot, therefore, always have regard to the unemployment to which a wage demand might give rise, as critics say they should or as others say they do. To say that the unions' 'sense of self-preservation, if not their *raison d'être*, demands that they keep in mind the economic welfare not only of their employed members but of all their members and even would-be members', is to ignore the difficult realities with which a union officer has to deal: how can he carry a policy which would sacrifice his members to lapsed members and to persons not only un-organized, but unknown? In fact, unions have sometimes felt it necessary to pursue policies, e.g. preservation of a standard, which carried with them some risks that some of their members would lose their jobs in consequence of them.

There have been outstanding examples in the history of the coal industry. The Royal Commission on the *Coal Industry* (*1925*) commented favourably on the two main principles of the miners' wage agreement of 1921:[2] there was a minimum wage which had to be paid irrespective of the economic conditions of the industry for the time being, whether the industry could afford it or not, representing the bare needs for subsistence or some standard of living which had been won, and which the miners thought should not be abandoned even at the cost of reducing the size of the industry and the numbers that could be employed. Secondly, there was an economic wage 'determined scientifically' on the basis of sharing

[1] H. M. Hallsworth. *The Shipbuilding Industry*. In, *Britain in Depression*. 1935. pp. 250–1; and in, *Britain in Recovery*. 1938. pp. 353–4. (Both prepared by Section F of the British Association for the Advancement of Science.)

[2] Rep. pp. 132–5, 163–4; 1926 Cmd. 2600, xiv.

the net proceeds of the industry, and fluctuating, as was necessary in an industry exposed (as it was then) to foreign competition and market fluctuations. By 1925–26 the industry was in a state of crisis, a 'disaster' was impending over the industry, and 'an immediate reduction of working costs was essential to save it'.[1] The mine owners had proposed that the gap between costs and proceeds should be bridged by an increase in the length of the working day, reductions of wages, etc. Before the Commission the miners made no proposals for dealing with the immediate situation, though the campaign of the Secretary, A. J. Cook, was summed up in the slogan 'not a penny off the pay, not a minute on the day'. The Commission took the view that the extension of hours in a depression was not a natural but an unnatural way of reducing costs, that the extension proposed would, if total output were unaltered, add 130,000 to the numbers already unemployed[2] (15 per cent in July 1925), or smaller numbers if the miners were prepared to agree to a combination of some reduction of wages and some extension of hours. This was the economic issue on which the difference of view between the miners and the General Council of the T.U.C. brought the General Strike of 1926 to an end and on which the miners remained out for so many disastrous months. The miners were resolute in their stand for no reductions of wages and no lengthening of the day, which the General Council, or at least some of its members, thought would make the size of the unemployment problem so large as to be unmanageable.[3]

The matter came up again in 1929. There were still 12·9 per cent of miners unemployed in January 1930, but the union pressed for a reduction of hours without decrease of pay, with the aim of

[1] Ibid. p. 236.
[2] Ibid. p. 173.
[3] There were also vital differences of opinion on procedure, on whether if a national strike were declared the T.U.C. took over the whole control or the miners had any autonomy left. Before the strike was called, Bevin declared, 'in twenty-four hours you may have to cease being separate unions for this purpose. You will have to become one union with no autonomy.' *The Mining Crisis and the National Strike, 1926.* T.U.C. Report. 1927. p. 16. How much autonomy the miners should have given up was one of the matters on which the split between the miners and the other unions occurred. The report is the best official source on the whole tangled story. The question came up again in the debate on a proposal for a joint national strike fund, made at T.U.C., Bournemouth, 1958. See speeches by Wigglesworth, September 2nd, and Webber, September 4th. pp. 337, 436.

work-sharing and on the ground that the miners should not be asked to pay for the reforms in the Coal Mines Act, 1930. The Act provided for organized marketing arrangements to maintain or raise the price of coal in the home market, but any economies from this source would take time to show themselves. The strength of the miners' demand for the re-establishment of the standards they had lost in 1926 thus led them to pursue a policy which offered, in the state of the market, little immediate prospect of work to those without it and perhaps risked increasing the number of them.[1] The attitude of those not in work cannot be discovered: 'work-sharing' would be attractive, and perhaps some supported the union's policy, for it could be regarded as a fight to insist that standards of living should be the last, not the first, source of reductions of costs and that in the long run the economies should be obtained through better organization.

Cases where the magnitude of the unemployment involved and the severity of the choice to be made between employment and maintaining standards were so great, have not been common, but there are milder ones. A union may sometimes regard the maintenance of an established differential as more important than any unemployment created through increased wage rates. In 1952–53, for fear of falling behind, the cotton unions presented a demand for higher wages even though unemployment was at 30 per cent.[2] And it was reported[3] that partly because of the rise of the Bank Rate and the fears of trade recession, eighteen building trade unions had decided to ask for a shorter working week of forty hours, and a rise of 8d. per hour, of which 5d. was to compensate for the fall of earnings through shorter hours. Here the desire to maintain

[1] In an understanding comment on the miners' dilemma H. Clay remarked: 'If hewers' wages for a full week could be brought down to the level of a pound a week, it would no doubt be possible to employ without loss not only all the miners at present employed, but also those who are unemployed: should their wages be brought down to that figure? On the other hand, a portion of the industry could be made to pay even on the 1924 basis; probably a half or more, instead of a quarter of the miners would be found out of employment. . . . Are there no limits to the range within which wages should be forced up or down? It appears to me that the only practical limits are the rough limits set by a comparison with the rates in other industries of the country.' H. Clay. *The Problem of Industrial Relations.* 1929. p. 180.

[2] H. A. Turner. *Inflation and Wage Differentials in Gt. Britain.* In, J. T. Dunlop. *The Theory of Wage Determination.* 1957. p. 128.

[3] *The Times.* Friday, Oct. 25th, 1957. p. 10c.

standards, coupled with a desire to share out work, led to a demand which would raise the price of labour at a time when it was feared that the demand for it would fall.

A somewhat different case, carefully set out by Dr. Sells,[1] occurred in the dressmaking trade, for which wage rates were negotiated through the Trade Board for dressmaking, bespoke tailoring and millinery trades. The dressmaking trade certainly contracted with great rapidity after the establishment of the Board's wage rates. Did the rates destroy the trade? There were some discharges in rural areas, and in 1921 the Ministry of Labour reported that in these areas 70 per cent of the inspections revealed evasions. In evidence before the Cave Committee[2] the Department said that it had doubts about enforcing the rates because they would have caused unemployment. But a large part of the trade was in any case doomed by the rise of competition from the machine-made product, which was cheaper and enabled women to see the final product before buying it. Drapers did not object, since it meant a transfer from their counters selling dressmaking materials to those selling ready-mades. Perhaps the right judgment is that the new rates led to the dressmakers being driven out faster than they would have been otherwise; and if one thinks of the long struggle of the handloom weavers a century earlier, no doubt the swifter process was the kinder. A similar instructive case was the competition of factory with outworkers in the linen and making-up trades of Northern Ireland.[3]

But suppose a union tries to fix both rates of pay and the numbers employed? In its dispute with Bournemouth Corporation, the Musicians' Union claimed before the Industrial Court that 'a proper object of a trade union is to establish by agreement with an employer the number of workers to be employed'. This was in line with its endeavour to get the Theatrical Managers' Association to agree to fix the number of musicians to be employed in each theatre and music hall, but the managers replied that they were not willing to agree 'to any proposal to fix the size, composition or quality of orchestras', matters 'solely within the discretion of the individual

[1] D. Sells. *The British Trade Boards System.* 1923. pp. 193–202.

[2] *Trade Board Acts.* Rep.; 1922 Cmd. 1645, x, 669. Mins. of ev.; 1922 Non-Parl., also *Breviate, 1917–1939.* p. 322.

[3] *Conditions of Employment in the Linen Trades of North of Ireland.* Cttee. Rep.; 1912–13 Cd. 6509, xxxiv, 365; also *Breviate, 1900–1916.* pp. 412–13.

managers concerned'; though some individual theatre managers did make such an agreement. The union said that it was mainly concerned to secure employment for its members against the competition of mechanically produced music and to prevent the reduction of opportunities for young musicians wishing to enter the profession, though they also had something to say about the balance of the orchestra between the various instruments. An interesting economic principle is involved. For if the employing authorities or firms must employ staff in pre-determined size groups, and cannot, whether for reasons of musical balance or otherwise, vary the composition of the group at will, then instead of any reduction of employment showing itself in the saving of a musician here and another there and so on, i.e. by marginal variations, it might take the form of a sudden substantial reduction of size or the disbandment of a particular orchestra. The Court did not accept the union's contention on the point, and in effect Bournemouth ceased to be the employing authority, financial responsibility being accepted by the authorities of the region and other bodies.[1]

In these cases the connection between wage rates and the level of employment stood out sharply, but in the kind of situation with which the unions normally have to deal other important factors may be operating. Unions can watch the situation only in a general way. The existence of unemployed members is less of a threat than it was in the early history of unions, when only the unions' modest out-of-work pay was immediately available. The establishment of the national insurance and assistance systems has weakened this threat, but even so, insurance benefit rates are below the wages, sometimes substantially below in most occupations, and there is some figure of unemployment which a union cannot disregard.[2] And, of course,

[1] Industrial Court. Award No. 2479. 1953.

[2] The years of overfull employment and inflation since 1945 seem to have made the unions less sensitive to the elasticity of demand for labour, so that in the stiffer economic conditions after the raising of the Bank Rate in September 1957, there were protests against any redundancy that might follow a wage rise demanded, e.g. when traffic was lagging or falling, as on railways and London buses, when unsold stocks were piling up, as in the coal industry, or when Government expenditure was reduced. For example, the Institute of Professional Civil Servants at its Conference in May 1958 condemned the Government instructions that pay increases should be offset by corresponding economies. *The Times*, May 20th, 1958, p. 5, col. 7.

there is the feeling of moral obligation which a union feels towards its unemployed members.

The effect on other workers

Secondly, the rise of plasterers' wages could be obtained at the expense of other factors of production by reducing theirs; the limits to that are set by their elasticity of supply. If it were elastic, the reduction of pay would cause a more than proportionate fall in the supply of those factors, which would in due course move or be diverted to other parts of the industrial field. Carpenters could, in some areas, move to work in the shipyards. Or the pay and number of non-operative workers—clerical, executive, administrative, technical—could be attacked. It has been claimed that they are too numerous, that their pay and conditions of work as to hours and paid holidays are unnecessarily better than those of manual workers, that the number of supervisory staff has grown unduly, etc.[1] Mrs. Webb took the view that the co-operative movement had shown that it was unnecessary to pay exhorbitant salaries to middle-class officials,[2] but later inquirers concluded that it had suffered by not attracting more people of the highest ability, for which purpose better prospects of promotion and financial incentives were desirable.[3] In the early stages of nationalization there were criticisms of excessive administrative costs, though the defence of the high salaries paid to the chairmen of the boards of nationalized industries that the best brains were needed to run concerns of this size was not, however, quite water-tight, since the demand for that type of capacity was itself partly the result of making the units bigger. But in 1956 the Herbert Committee on the *Electricity Supply Industry* complained of the conditions which were causing well-qualified men of the calibre of potential leaders to turn away from the industry, and wanted improvements in conditions of tenure, promotion prospects and differentials, as well as the creation of more posts of

[1] In the man-hours paid for but not worked (mainly holidays) there is a differential in favour of administrative, etc., employees. The total social security contribution, including private pension schemes, is £40 18s. 1d. for miners and £106 7s. 2d. for administrative staff. *Ministry of Labour Gazette*, Aug. 1957. pp. 278–9.

[2] B. Potter (Mrs. Webb). *The Co-operative Movement*. 1891. pp. 214–15.

[3] A. M. Carr-Saunders, P. S. Florence and R. Peers. *Consumer's Co-operation in Great Britain*. 1938. pp. 321, 326–7. See also Co-operative Independent Commission Report, Co-operative Union, Ltd. 1958. pp. 65–7.

responsibility;[1] and the Fleck Committee on the reorganization of the National Coal Board's machinery concluded that executive heads of big headquarters' departments should have a salary of £7,500 and that those of full-time members of the Board should be substantially increased.[2] In addition, account has to be taken of the existence of unions at the upper wage and salary levels. Carpenters do not accept a cut or 'move elsewhere' just to please plasterers; even before the Federation was established there was some understanding, and there must now be some agreement between the constituent unions as to what these relative rates should be. In other industries there may be unions of technicians and other workers in the higher wage and salary grades whose function is to stand up for the rights of their own members. It is clear from the wage claims made by clerical, executive and professional workers that they are not willing to allow their position relatively to that of operative workers to be whittled away if they can avoid it.

Raising wages at the expense of profits

What proportions of the dividends of shareholders are open to attack and transfer to the pay packet? The result of attempts to eat into the payment of capital would depend on its elasticity of supply, and in an individual industry could obviously have a measure of success in the short run, for much capital is immobile and cannot be withdrawn or diverted to other uses if the payment for it is diminished. For some kinds of undertakings initial capital costs are high and maintenance costs low; in such cases, as investors in some overseas enterprises have discovered, they may be able to run on a long time without paying any or sufficient dividends to attract fresh capital. In others, continual supplies of fresh capital may be needed.

In the long run new supplies of capital can be diverted to other industries, so that the trouble comes when more is wanted. To the engineering unions, which had argued before the Court of Inquiry in 1956 that the total distributed in net dividends after tax was two and three-quarter times greater in 1956 than in 1950, the employers replied that in 1953–55 the total additional capital invested for the purposes they specified was £730 million and that this accounted for and was attracted by the increased total dividend

[1] Rep. pp. 84, 144; 1955–56 Cmd. 9672, xv.
[2] *Organization*. Adv. Cttee. Rep. p. 17. National Coal Bd., 1955.

payments.[1] In the last few years the amount of capital put into the coal industry each year has been nearly equal to the total sum of £160 million paid for all the coal mines when they were nationalized, and the plan implies an expenditure of perhaps £1,200 million[2] in fifteen years. Obtaining fresh supplies on this scale is not a costless process: the problem of raising and paying for them would remain even if the coal mines had been confiscated and had therefore cost nothing. It would remain even if, as the Guild Socialists had proposed, each Guild Industry paid out of its revenues an annual rent to the State to be used, amongst other things, as a source of supply of new capital, for it would then have that much less to distribute to its workers. Then something above the common run of profit—the amount depending on investors' attitude to risk and their current mood—usually has to be paid to secure sufficient capital when there are considerable risks of loss through unforeseen events. That such risks are a reality and not just the results of capitalists' miscalculations was brought home sharply to those too uncritical in their belief in the efficiency of the State in trading, by the millions lost on the ground nuts scheme.[3]

The amount of dividends open to attack thus lies between a short run upper limit, when little or sometimes nothing need be paid, and a long run lower limit set by the cost of obtaining fresh supplies of capital, including where necessary a risk payment. How much higher dividends are than this minimum level is not a question open to general answer. The possibilities of raising wages at their expense are obviously narrower in one industry taken by itself, since alternative fields lie open to investors. But if unions are active in all industries, the capital cannot be 'diverted', and the question is then whether the dividends remaining are enough to induce sufficient supplies of capital in total to come forward, for those who save have the alternative of consuming instead of saving. Thus an aspect of an old discussion, whether a zero rate of interest is possible, comes forward again with some practical relevance. There is no doubt

---

[1] *Engineering and Allied Employers' National Federation and ... the Confederation of Shipbuilding and Engineering Unions. Dispute.* Ct. of Inquiry. Rep. p. 11; 1956–57 Cmnd. 159, xiv.

[2] E. F. Schumacher. 'Britain's Coal.' In, *National Provincial Bank Review,* Nov. 1957.

[3] *Public Accounts.* Sel. Cttee. 2nd Rep. pp. v, vi, xi. Evidence of L. Plummer and Final Evidence of F. Lee; 1950 (70) iii. Also *The Future of the Overseas Food Corporation;* 1950–51 Cmd. 8125, xxvii.

some element of convention in the actual rate necessary to induce saving in the sense that savers can in time get used to pitching their expectations of reward in a lower key. But the convention takes time to change and the ultimate risk is therefore that of increasing wages at a pace which would press the net yield of investment below what was the conventional minimum at the moment. This point is taken up later (p. 84). How far wage increases can come out of profits in conditions of full employment and inflation is discussed on pp. 118, 119.

It has occasionally been suggested, e.g. by the Confederation of Shipbuilding and Engineering Unions in presenting their case before a Court of Inquiry, that some use could be made of companies' reserves for wage increases. This drew from the Court the following comment: 'We do not think in the main that the form of the reserves is such that they could be drawn upon for that purpose; for the bulk of the reserves had been and were being used in re-equipping and replacing plant, machinery and buildings and keeping them up to date, etc. A rise of wage is normally a permanent charge, and it is to future earning power that regard must be had when considering whether any increase in wages can be borne out of profits.'[1] The Cohen Council argued that ploughing back profits for physical growth and research was one of the means by which businesses have always grown, that in 1939 company savings were half the size of total savings by individuals, and that in a period of inflation it was necessary to provide in this way for the increased cost of carrying stock-in-trade and work in progress and for replacing fixed assets at higher prices. They expressed the view that unless it had been done, it would have been impossible to raise in the open market the capital necessary to finance the investment which had taken place. The practice might sometimes be carried to excess, when it might have been better if more had been distributed to shareholders so that they could invest in other lines of industry.[2]

(ii) *Raising wages at the expense of the consumer*

Thirdly, the price of labour could be raised at the expense of the consumer. In Marshall's example, this would depend on the

[1] *Engineering and Allied Employers' National Federation and ... the Confederation of Shipbuilding and Engineering Unions. Dispute.* Ct. of Inquiry. Rep. pp. 31, 46, 47; 1953–54 Cmd. 9084, xv.

[2] Council, Prices, Productivity and Incomes. First Rep. paras. 153–8, and Conclusion 33; 1958. Non-Parl.

elasticity of demand for building work, e.g. house room. People can rent smaller houses, young people setting up can stay in rooms a little longer before taking a house, people buying houses can let one floor for a bit instead of occupying it wholly themselves. All these adjustments are daily visible. The price of articles of inelastic demand purchased by wealthy groups, such as Court dress, could be pushed up to provide more wages for those who make them, though the increased hiring of ceremonial, men's evening and other formal dress seems to indicate not only an extension of convention to new and lower income groups, but also of an alternative being exercised by groups who formerly would have bought.

Again, if the employer, say a great trustified industry, has a monopoly of a product or line of products, a union's pressure can make him share with them the spoils of its exploitation of the consumer. An early example of this was the Birmingham Bedstead Alliance of 1890, whereby a manufacturers' association with a binding price list made a formal agreement with the unions to employ only union members, and to pay certain wage rates, in return for union undertakings to supply workers only to members of the association and to support the employers against any firm breaking away from the association.[1] But the power to obtain such gains depends on whether one union or many are operating on this policy. Even if its members consume some of the commodity they produce, one union acting alone can certainly gain by pressing a wage claim which may push up its price at the expense of all the other consumers. A 10 per cent rise in money wage might thus give the members nearly a 10 per cent rise in real wages. But if a postal worker's wage claim, a coal miner's wage claim, a railway worker's wage claim, a road transport wage claim and so on, are each passed on to the consumer, in due course the unions' members would begin to lose as consumers some of what they had gained as trade unionists. Not quite as much, because that portion of the population with fixed incomes or not organized into bargaining groups or not covered by statutory regulation would lose by the rise of prices without sharing the gains. It is, indeed, the existence of persons not participating in the gains which makes the process pay those who do.

[1] J. A. Hobson. *Evolution of Modern Capitalism*. Revised ed. 1906. pp. 171–2.

(iii) *Raising wages by improved industrial efficiency*

Finally, unions have always argued that a major source of wage increases is to be found in improvements in the technological and business efficiency of firms and industries. The rise in real standards must have been brought about largely in this way, since until after 1945 at least, only a modest fraction of the national income was redistributed through social security payments and services. The commonly quoted figure of 3 per cent for annual increase in production is but an average of various rates of advance in the separate industries, and the gains in real standards of the workers in any one of them are due not only to its own technological advances, but to those which take place in all the other industries. Trade union arguments on this point, as set out in speeches and in evidence supporting wage claims, have been one of three: if substantial technological advances are being made in the industry concerned, that the workers should share in the benefits; if a reduction of wages is being asked for by the employers, that every possible step should first be taken to improve organization and efficiency as speedily as circumstances allow, since reductions in the wage bill should be the last, not the first source of economy; if the union is demanding a rise, that insistence upon it would spur laggard employers to mechanize and in other ways to improve their organization so that they could afford to pay it. The most notable example is to be found in the evidence of the miners before the Commissions of 1919 and 1925, which reviewed exhaustively a large number of possible improvements in technology and organization. Some of these suggestions were repeated and many others added in the report of the Reid Technical Advisory Committee on *Coal Mining*, 1945.[1] And, translated into the appropriate technologies, they can be generalized to apply to other industries. For example: 'It might be that some very inefficient firms would have some difficulty in meeting the additional cost, but the country could not afford backwardness and inefficiency in industry, nor could the unions be expected to encourage it by withholding a justified and necessary claim'.[2] Pressure

[1] 1944–45 Cmd. 6610, iv.

[2] *Engineering and Allied Employers' National Federation and ... the Confederation of Shipbuilding and Engineering Unions. Dispute.* Ct. of Inquiry. Rep. para. 43; 1953–54 Cmd. 9084, xv.

on backward employers was specifically part of the basis of an engineering claim.[1]

To be a source of better wages, the improvements must not only lead to an increased physical output, but pay their cost. For they imply new machinery, new equipment or new factory lay-out, and these mean more capital; and the savings, which depend on the number of units of product and the saving on each unit, must cover the capital cost. Not all modernizations proposed pass these tests. The Working Party on *Light Clothing* pointed out that high-speed machines are economical for some processes, but not for others.[2] Fully automatic and semi-automatic machinery in pottery manufacture would increase output per man-hour, but would not revolutionize costs, so that despite a reduction in the number of operatives from eight to four, the interest and depreciation charges would be such that the net savings would be not more than one penny per dozen plates and might disappear in the making of larger plates.[3] In lace manufacture there had been a very limited number of technical advances in twenty-five years, many machines fifty years old were working well if they had been systematically cared for, and little was to be gained by immediate re-equipment.[4] The fact that a certain level of output was necessary to justify the cost of installing labour-saving machinery in cabinet making led in some directions to a tendency to seek volume for volume's sake, at the expense of design.[5] In the boot and shoe industry most of the machinery is obtained from one firm, whose practice of leasing it for a fixed or output-basis rent had resulted in a high standard of mechanization and replacement: the complaints were about 'tied' leases and their effect in keeping out competing machinery-makers.[6] The Platt Mission reported that a substantial portion of the machinery in the cotton industry was not only old in type, but beyond its efficient working life,[7] though some dissenting members of the Cotton Working Party pointed out that timing and highly selective mechanization were important if costs were not actually to be increased.

[1] Title, see n. 2, p. 66. Rep. para. 27, ix; 1956–57 Cmnd. 159, xix.
[2] Rep. p. 29; 1947 Non-Parl. Bd. of Trade.
[3] *Pottery.* Working Party. Rep. p. 13; 1946 Non-Parl.
[4] *Lace.* Working Party. Rep. p. 143; 1947 Non-Parl.
[5] *Furniture.* Working Party. Rep. p. 89; 1946 Non-Parl.
[6] *Boots and Shoes.* Working Party. Rep. pp. 15, 16; 1946 Non-Parl.
[7] *Cotton.* Working Party. Rep. pp. 66, 226–30; 1946 Non-Parl.

And it is sometimes possible to increase mechanization without expensive equipment; e.g. by reorganizing weaving sheds so that each weaver, instead of working four, could operate six, eight or more Lancashire looms.[1] Then a distinction must be drawn between mechanization which economizes in labour or in other ways, and mechanization undertaken simply because some other factor, e.g. labour, has become more costly.[2]

On the other hand, the economies of machinery can sometimes be lost through undue restrictions imposed by the unions on its introduction and use. In the nineteenth century the handloom weavers tried to beat the new machines by cutting their own earnings and standards. The alternative tradition built up by the unions was to try to regulate their introduction by consultations about the number and type of workers to be employed and the wage rates which were appropriate, and a great deal of such discussion now takes place continually. But there are cases where the restraints make labour so costly that the employers' incentive to install the machine is weakened or frustrated. Webb noted an early case in 1894, when the Leicester branch of the Boot and Shoe Operatives' Union demanded a price list which would have left the employers with no incentive to introduce the machines, just as the employers' terms would have given the workmen no incentive to use them.[3] The Cotton Manufacturing Commission pointed out that the wages system (the Uniform List, originated in 1892) hindered mechanization in that whatever steps the employer took to enable his workers to increase their output, the wage cost per unit remained the same; it provided too little reward for efficient and inadequate penalties for inefficient management.[4] Between 1927 and 1939 much work was done in the mines to mechanize the coal face and improve the roadways, with only an 11 per cent gain in output per man shift.[5] The very bad relations between miners and owners after the stoppage of 1926 were not conducive to willing co-operation by the men, and 'when machinery was installed, its potential savings seem largely to have been dissipated by the quiet but effective determination of the men

[1] Ibid. p. 234.

[2] Ibid. p. 228.

[3] S. and B. Webb. *Industrial Democracy*. 1902. pp. 401–2.

[4] *Cotton Manufacturing Industry*. Com. Interim Rep. pp. 15, 16. Also pp. 5, 11; 1948 Non-Parl. Min of Labour.

[5] *Coal Mining*. Technical Advisory Cttee. Rep.; 1944–45 Cmd. 6610, iv.

that the number of men discharged should be kept as low as possible', and their steadfast requirement that inappropriate old customs and traditions should be observed. This put a brake on the modernization of the industry.[1] Again, it was said that dock workers had insisted on such wages and other terms that it was unprofitable to use a machine. The Working Party on *Increased Mechanization in the U.K. Ports* reported that the men took the view that the financial gains from new machines should be shared between employers and workpeople. 'We have found little evidence of appreciation by the workpeople of the further point that the increased use of machinery is required not for financial gain to employers or employees, but rather to see that an economy is made which will . . . affect the fortunes of the nation and individual consumer of the goods they handle by a reduction in freight rates and a general lowering of handling charges.'[2] The Shawcross Commission on *The Press* concluded that in four national newspaper offices, on account of over-manning, use of 'ghost' workers and failure to exploit new machinery and techniques fully, there was a surplus of 34 per cent in manpower.[3] The shipbuilding industry has been bedevilled with demarcation disputes which have prevented delivery at due date.[4]

The opportunities of unions to increase wages by pressing for mechanization thus vary from industry to industry: there may be little room for technical improvement for a time, or the level of mechanization may already be very high or the machines such that their cost eats up all the savings they make. And if a union's claim that the gains must be shared between employers and workers is such that nothing is left for reductions of costs, this could only mean that the benefits of the inventions were restricted to the people in the trade concerned. As inventions do not take place evenly throughout industry, there would be inequalities between the groups of workers, for, as we have seen, the rise of real standards of life in any one industry depend not only on its own technical developments, but on those taking place in other industries and passed on

[1] Ibid. p. 15.
[2] Rep. p. 7; 1950 Non-Parl. Min. of Transport.
[3] *The Press*. R. Com. Rep. paras. 86–96, summary of conclusions, paras. 24–9, and App. XII; 1961–62 Cmnd. 1811.
[4] Shipbuilding Advisory Cttee. Rep. of Sub. Cttee. on *Prospects* pp. 10–11; 1961, Non-Parl.

by price reductions. Such a policy of 'complete sharing' between employers and workers would thus be advantageous to those working in industries happening to be in a phase of technical progress, but the others would not gain. Since, for example, there was no revolutionary and fundamental alteration in the methods of the building trade for a long period up to 1914 and perhaps in some ways even to 1939, the application of the principle that technical gains should be retained by the industries in which they took place would have deprived its workers of part of their rise of real standards.

Finally, for mechanization capital is required. Though there were great differences in the financial returns to investment between different colleries, the chronic unprofitability of coal mining as a whole from 1929–38, when the average profit was no more than 7d. per ton, could not have been conducive to a great inflow of capital for improvements. In the pottery industry, tunnel kilns produced savings far greater than the actual savings in fuel costs, but their installation required large-scale rebuilding and alterations. The average profit on turnover in the industry for 1923–38 was only 4 per cent, and since out of 200 firms only seven consistently made a profit in the region of 10 per cent on turnover, a substantial number of firms had a poor financial record. The Working Party felt that 4 per cent return need not deter borrowers or lenders from financing improvements, provided they were selective, and if they could get long-term loans.[1]

No doubt many great schemes of mechanization and modernization could be undertaken if ample supplies of capital could be had for little or nothing. But the rate of interest, though it guides new capital into industries the demand for whose products makes them profitable enough to pay it, rather than into those which might be regarded by some as desirable on this or that social ground, at least limits the amount lent to the total available. When therefore unions (or employers—or 'working parties' on industries) contend that this or that industry could modernize if sufficient capital were available at specially low rates, this is of course true. But it implies that some other industries productive enough to pay the rate would have to make do with less capital than they could profitably use. In order to give employers a fillip to be more optimistic,[2] Professor

---

[1] *Pottery.* Working Party. Rep. pp. 3, 6–7; 1946 Non-Parl.
[2] *Cotton.* Working Party. Rep. p. 229; 1946 Non-Parl.

Jewkes was, however, willing to concede an offer to the cotton industry at a low rate of interest, provided the amount was not excessive and that it was temporary.

What scope for wage increases is to be found in improvements in the organization of the factory and in the environment of the worker? In this field also a wide range of suggestions has been advanced by unions in the course of wage claims and disputes. Before the Samuel Commission the miners charged the owners with numerous deficiencies of organization, such as shortages of tubs, rails, timber, etc., which adversely affected output and therefore earnings, though the Commission thought that the effect on output was exaggerated.[1] Then unions have continually criticized the inefficiency of weak, marginal managements on the ground that their productivity was low and that wages could be raised if they were eliminated or if the efficiency of the worst were brought up to the level of the average or the best. The Working Party on *Boots and Shoes* pointed out that in firms making men's cheap grade footwear, for example, the productivity per operative per annum varied from 720 to 1,440 pairs, the net value of output from £111 to £247,[2] and that there was a very wide range between the highest and the lowest average earnings of piece-work operatives in different establishments of the same size and in the same district. Thus, in factories of 201–500 operatives, the difference between the highest and lowest was in Leicester 4*d*. per operative-hour, in Northampton nearly 10*d*. These differences, the report suggested, arose more from variations in the efficiency of operation of the factories than from any other cause.

The unions' refusal to listen to the pleas of weak firms that they could not afford to pay the same rates as stronger firms is intended to present them with the choice of improving or being eliminated by competition. Though this policy may have some effect in both ways, yet in one sense the problem is insoluble. For though the development of rules and techniques of management which can be 'picked up' or formally learned may perhaps enable the less naturally efficient managers to bring up some of their routines to a higher level, managerial ability is not evenly distributed amongst the population, but like height, weight, etc., must lie on a bell-shaped curve, with a few of the ablest, a few of the worst and many just

[1] *Coal Industry* (*1925*). R. Com. Rep. p. 230; 1926 Cmd. 2600, xiv.
[2] Rep. pp. 21–3, 81–7; 1946 Non-Parl. Bd. of Trade.

F

above and below 'average'. The selection and training of managers and executives in nationalized industries presents a special problem. It was long ago observed by Marshall that whereas in conditions of competition a young and able man could get experience in wider and varied fields of responsibility by the growth of his own firm or by moving from smaller to larger undertakings, when an industry came under one control he could do this only by formal promotion, and his opportunities and training might both be narrowed.[1] The reality of this danger was confirmed by the Herbert Committee on the *Electricity Supply Industry* (1956),[2] which was seriously concerned with the industry's policy of not earmarking individuals for particular jobs and failing to practice selective posting. It even favoured putting 'unseen tabs' on bright young men, saying that there was no substitute for a deliberate scheme by which men were carefully selected, trained and advanced in particular posts so that they emerged in middle life as potential leaders of the industry. At the other end of the scale, schemes for the systematic training of the semi-skilled and unskilled in the plant, as distinct from unorganized methods by which inexperienced workers learn to do their jobs by working alongside more experienced men under the general supervision of foremen, are apparently difficult to find in Britain outside textiles, garment making and lamp and valve manufacture. Employers apparently feel that the large labour turnover of these workers which occurs in full employment makes such training unprofitable, while the breakdown of jobs into simple operations makes it unnecessary.[3]

At an earlier stage, as in the case of the match girls who went on strike in 1888 and of workers first brought under the Trades Boards, in some industries wages and standards of life were so low that nutrition and clothing were quite inadequate for maintaining health and physical vigour, so that increased wages made for better health and efficiency, and thus 'justified' and 'made possible' higher wages. This was the argument not only of trade unions, but also of 'model employers'. Little need be added to Pigou's suggestions that in these cases the beneficial effects on efficiency depended on how low the wages were to start with, i.e. how much room there was for improvement of standards, and on holding the higher wages long

---

[1] A. Marshall. *Industry and Trade.* 1923. pp. 660–2.
[2] Rep. pp. 320–8; 1955–56 Cmd. 9672, xv.
[3] *Ministry of Labour Gazette.* May 1957. pp. 282–3.

enough to enable ill-fed and ill-clothed workers to build up a new standard of life. And it is worth remembering that in 1890 the sweated immigrant boot and shoe finishers of London, who worked in appalling conditions in the homes of immigrant masters who had preceded them into the country, went on strike to be taken into factories.[1] Personal inefficiency of workers through underfeeding due to low wages or unemployment must now be reduced to small proportions by the rise in wages and the social services, while the improvement in the workshop environment is visible in the modern factory. Anyone who remembers walking in Bow or Bethnal Green, say, at the time the Trades Boards were set up, and followed the same route to-day could not fail to see the improvement out of all knowledge of the dress, health and feeling of well-being of the inhabitants. Yet to those brought up on the text-book histories of continually advancing factory legislation, the conditions still existing in some of the older Lancashire factories revealed in Margaret McCarthy's *Generation in Revolt* (1953) were something of a shock. The Committee on the Health of Munition Workers[2] showed how much there was to learn at that date on the organization of work, rest, lighting and temperatures, etc., as a means of improving efficiency, and though the gap between knowledge and practice was perhaps greater then than it is now, one need not suppose that knowledge in this field will cease to grow; and in any case contemporary practice is uneven as between factory and factory. According to a Ministry of Labour survey, of 578 boot and shoe factories, 387 had insufficient washing accommodation, though 323 had space available without loss of production space; 103 had bad daylight lighting, and 112 needed extensive improvements in artificial lighting. Similar conditions occur in other 'old' industries, such as lace making, pottery and furniture making,[3] still in a state of transition to modern methods. The Working Party reports on all four industries asked for a vigorous enforcement of the Factory Acts.

[1] *The Times*. Mar. 31st, 1890. p. 6d.; all issues Apr. 1st–8th, especially Apr. 8th, p. 10, col. a.; Apr. 10th, 15th, 16th, 18th, 28th.
[2] Reports; 1917–18 Cd. 8511, xvi. 1918 Cd. 9065, xii; also *Breviate, 1900–1916.* p. 198.
[3] *Lace*. Working Party. Rep. pp. 114–17; 1947 Non-Parl. *Pottery*. Working Party. Rep. pp. 4, 5; 1946 Non-Parl. 'The problem of the slum factory is now acute.' *Furniture*. Working Party. Rep. p. 93; 1946 Non-Parl. '... The 1937 Factories Act makes no effective provision for the elimination of this type of factory.'

In these questions of organization the main responsibility for initiative must rest with the employers, but other factors are more within the workers' control. It is obvious that a great deal depends on his zest for the job. It seems doubtful whether in one or two industries this is as great here as in the U.S.A.—building and mining are said to be examples—and, indeed, if one watches Italian building workers there would seem to be little doubt that a comparison would not be favourable to us.[1] But this involves questions of personal and social attitudes. A reduction of absenteeism would obviously raise productivity: a steady 5 per cent of absenteeism means that the staff must be about 5 per cent larger to get the same output. Some of it is involuntary, arising from general causes such as illness and domestic circumstances, some may be reducible by improvement in factory conditions, but some is certainly voluntary. But part of the voluntary absenteeism is a consequence of greatly improved wages, for the purchase of extra leisure by sacrifice of pay is then both a possible and may be a natural choice. But to set against this is the fact that it is known that numbers of workers, under the inducement of piece or overtime rates, are putting in very long hours, though it is not yet known how extensive the practice is. It is also possible to find workers with short hours who have second jobs, and many with five-day week manage to get odd jobs at the week-end.

(iv) *Speeding up the laggard employer*

Setting out the possible gains from improvements does not, however, put them into the pay packet. The theory is that insistence on a wage claim can jerk a firm or industry into improvements which would enable it to pay the increases. The 'jerk' is a sharp rise of costs to which an employer will try to respond by changing his processes and methods, but as the examples we have reviewed show, his freedom of manoeuvre may be great or small. In some firms and industries there may be substantial scope for improvement, e.g. when they are in uneven stages of transition from old to

---

[1] *Boots and Shoes.* Working Party. Rep. p. 25; 1946 Non-Parl. 'One very important reason for the high productivity of the U.S. industry lies in the psychological approach of the operative to his work. . . . It is not so much that the factors listed above cause the operative to work fast, but rather that those factors enable the operatives to fulfil their one clear object, namely, to earn as much as they can.'

fundamentally new methods, and a jerk may hasten the swing-over. In others there may be little room, because they are already running at a high level of mechanization and efficiency, or because no fundamental advances beyond the established techniques are yet in sight. Then improvements which give a greater physical output for a given physical effort are real increases of efficiency, but others are merely substitutes for labour which has become unduly expensive. Mechanization undertaken to evade the pressure of high wages has to be distinguished from mechanization which makes higher wages possible. One has therefore to think of each industry at any given moment as having a scale of possible improvements in technique or organization, beginning with small ones near-by present methods and rising to more and more fundamental changes involving fixed installations or more or less drastic re-organization. The scale may be graded in continual small steps, or a far-reaching change may be on the doorstep awaiting entry. Their cost has also to be considered: at the lower end of the scale there may be a wide range of small changes of low cost but cumulatively important, followed further up by substantial improvements in technique or organization which may be technically productive but initially expensive. Or the alternative methods available may yield such modest economies that they will be used only if labour has become dearer. Then union pressure on one of a number of competing firms may present it with the alternative of reducing costs in other ways or of being slowly eliminated. But if a redistribution of output from weak to strong firms caused in this way is not sufficient to enable an industry taken as a whole to meet a union claim, and there is not much room for technical improvement, it may then have to raise the prices of its products and thus risk reducing its sales. The effectiveness of a 'jerk' depends a great deal on the technical and cost circumstances of each industry. The possibilities are too varied to be covered adequately by the simple phrase 'overcoming employers' inertia by a jolt'—especially as unions themselves may also exhibit inertia and even resistance.

It does not always follow that 'improvements' which lead to an increase of output will increase wage-paying capacity at the time they are made. If the 'bottom has dropped out of the market', if the market is 'saturated', or, more generally, if demand is inelastic, increased output, even though obtained by better technique and organization, might produce a more than proportionate decrease of price and so lead to decreased, and not increased, aggregate proceeds to the industry. Thus in 1921 the mining industry raised 230 million tons of coal, of an aggregate value of £397 million, but in 1922, tonnage of 250 million was worth only £220 million; this, of course, was the result of deflation. In 1924 the tonnage raised was 267 million, in 1925, 248 million; but the aggregate value dropped from £252 million to £213 million and net value per ton from 18·18s. to 16·52s.[1] Finally, schemes of reorganization often take time to yield their fruits. Speaking of the £171 million invested by the Coal Board between 1947 and 1956 in major colliery reconstructions and new sinkings, etc., Mr. Schumacher says that 'it takes about ten years to sink a new colliery, and eight to carry through a major reconstruction. For this reason, a considerable part of the capital invested is still "in the pipe line", that is, spent on schemes not yet completed. So far, completed schemes account for about one-seventh of the total or £25 million.'[2] This is, of course, a period of exceptional length, but examples with shorter gestation periods are common enough. It may well be that in some of the nationalized industries the unions have asked for wage increases before the economies have been realized, or have not been content to see them passed on to the consumer in lower prices, but have succeeded in retaining the lion's share of the benefits for themselves.

5. WAGE INCREASES WITHOUT UNEMPLOYMENT

So far we have examined the conditions in which a union could secure an increase of wages per head and in the aggregate, though at the expense of restricting the expansion of employment or dislodging from the industry men who might either remain unemployed, or obtain work in 'near-by' industries at somewhat lower rates of pay, or be taken on in new expanding industries. But are there any circumstances in which a union could raise wages without creating any unemployment at all? In which, to use a phrase commonly employed in negotiations, a wage increase can be 'absorbed' without affecting prices or employment? First, a rise of money wage which merely offset currency expansion, when the prices of products and stocks are all rising, would not of itself give rise to unemployment. Secondly, as we have seen, wages can be raised by reducing the

[1] *Coal Industry (1925)*. R. Com. Mins. of ev. Vol. 3, p. 3; 1926 Non-Parl.
[2] E. F. Schumacher. 'Britain's Coal.' In, *National Provincial Bank Review*, Nov. 1957.

payment for capital below the market rate when it is immobile, until money for replacements and renewals is required. In some industries the extent of short-run immobility is such that firms can carry on for a considerable time paying no dividends and even slowly running down in efficiency; in others the commitment in fixed capital or business organization geared to specific purposes is limited and the short run may be short indeed: their costs may, for example, be largely costs of materials. Next, the industry may be expanding, and its sales proceeds increasing through a rise in the demand for its products. Then our review of the opportunities opened by improvements in technology and efficiency shows three ways in which it could be done. Some opportunities may come the way of the union without any effort on its part, by invention and the enterprise of the management; others, probably fewer, by the pressure it can exercise on laggard and inefficient employers. If these employers are able to respond by improved organization and methods, or are compelled by competition to yield business to more efficient ones, a wage rate could be fixed which did not decrease the total volume of employment, but transferred it from the less to the more efficient firms. The third is by raising wages which have been too low, so that the workers could develop better standards of nutrition, clothing and recreation; and so improve their personal efficiency as to make it profitable to employ them at a higher wage. This would seem to be the lesson of the early Trades Boards, which certainly contributed to a great improvement in basic standards.

There are two other possibilities to be added, both perhaps of historical rather than current significance. First, if there is an over-supply of labour in a particular industry large enough to depress earnings, the condition for raising them is that the surplus labour is diverted to some other part of the industrial field. If this can be done, earnings may be raised without decreasing the volume of employment. This is the oft-cited case of the dockers, who before 1914 were taken on by casual methods, the foremen picking out men twice or thrice daily as required from jostling crowds of men at the call stands—something like 30,000 men seeking for and 20,000 obtaining work in London.[1] As most of the work did not require specialized skill, it was open not only to 'regular' dockers and their families, but to unemployed building trade workers,

[1] H. A. Mess. *Casual Labour at the Docks*. 1916. p. 17.

seamen tired of the sea and seeking shore jobs, discharged soldiers, men thrown out of work from furniture making and french polishing, agricultural labourers, etc. Because engagements were casual, low wages showed themselves not so much in low rates per hour as in irregular earnings and too few shifts per man. The various efforts of the unions to raise the wage per shift, commencing with the strike for the 'dockers' tanner' in 1889, were no solution and often did little more than attract fresh recruits and so lower the number of shifts per man. The 54,000 dockers in London in 1914 rose, after the Shaw award of 16s. per day in 1919, to 61,000. The shipowners wanted enough men to enable them to cope with irregular ship arrivals and emergencies, which meant that a margin of men would in any case be under-employed. The men's interests, on the other hand, lay in having a smaller number of men with as near full-time work as possible, and some guaranteed maintenance for the margin of under-employed, but this could not be achieved without decasualization and the exclusion of many men from employment in order to keep down the size of the margin to a manageable number. The union's patient and hard struggle with its own members, who realized that some would be dislodged from the occupation, remains a largely untold but honourable story of constructive union policy.[1] The relevance of the story here is that by decasualization earnings per man could be raised without diminishing the volume of employment, but by decreasing the number of persons taken on to share it.

Secondly, there may be cases in which employers are able to obtain a sufficient number of workers at lower rates than they would be willing to pay to employ that number. If so, the union would be able to raise wages; but since such a situation means that the employers must be getting an extra bit of profit above what was necessary to induce them to maintain the volume of employment, why shouldn't they all try to expand and, by competition for workers, raise the wage until the extra profit disappeared? Examples of this situation occurred in miscellaneous industries engaged in

[1] The story can be picked up from H. A. Mess. op. cit. *Port Labour*. Cttee. Rep.; 1931 Non-Parl. Min. of Labour. P. Ford. *Work and Wealth in a Modern Port*. 1934. pp. 69–82. F. G. Hanham. *Casual Labour in the Merseyside Area*. 1930. E. C. P. Lascelles and S. S. Bullock. *Dock Labour and Decasualization*. 1924. *Port Transport Industry, Operation of the Dock Workers (Regulation of Employment) Scheme. 1947*. Cttee. Rep.; 1955–56 Cmd. 9813, xxvi. *Ocean Shipowners' Tally Clerks*. Cttee. Rep.; 1960, Non-Parl.

food preparation in the East End of London in World War I. The labour of many such factories consisted largely of local married women who accepted low rates because the work was conveniently near their homes, and there was a long lag in their poor wage— despite other opportunities of war work a little 'less local'—until the unions negotiated higher, sometimes doubled rates. Such workers often trooped into the union when negotiations were afoot, and trooped out again soon after the rise was obtained. There was no question of the factories expanding or of new ones being set up, because work on munitions was swallowing up other labour. Where, as in the case of some of the trades covered by the early Trades Boards, by reason of an excess of local labour the wages were also below those earned by equivalent workers in other indus- tries, one must suppose that the employers did not enlarge their staffs, although they might apparently have gained by doing so, because of their own inefficiency, lack of knowledge and resources. But over-supply of labour of either this or the first type occurred 'before the days of full employment', and although there may still be pockets of localized over-supply of labour, they must have greatly diminished and their chances of continuing on any scale have been much reduced by full employment.

6. TRADE UNIONS IN MORE THAN ONE TRADE

What are the effects of the migration or diversion of labour to other industries? The bulk of the workers of some crafts may be occupied in two industries: e.g. joiners and carpenters in the building and shipbuilding industries, engineers in the shipbuilding and engineering industries, plumbers in building and shipbuilding, while craftsmen of each type are found also in many industries engaged on the repair and maintenance of plant and buildings.

These facts suggest a way in which for the purposes of analysis we can construct a simplified version of such a situation which is recognizably like the actual one. We can, following Zeuthen, consider two trades only, 'of equal size', in which both the numbers employed are equal, and the wage rates are equal. Suppose that in one of these industries a union obtains a rise of pay, while in the other the labour market is still competitive, so that no restrictions are placed on the entry of new workers. The numbers and propor- tion of men dislodged from the unionized market will, as we have seen, depend on the elasticity of demand for their labour. If in due course these migrate to the second industry, they will increase the numbers of and competition between the workers seeking employment in it and tend to reduce the wages below the previous level. By how much?

The simplest situation is one in which the elasticity of demand for the workers in both trades is 1·0, i.e. in which a given percentage rise or fall of the wage rate will mean an equal percentage decrease or increase in the numbers employed; in that case, whatever the wage rate and numbers employed, the aggregate amount received in wages will be constant. In such conditions the rise of pay in the unionized industry will reduce the numbers employed in it so that the total wages received are unaltered. The transfer of workers will reduce the wage per head of both existing and added workers in the non-unionized industry below the original level in such a way that the total amount received in wages will also remain unaltered, and (since the markets are equal in size) will also be the same as in the unionized industry. Thus, those still in the unionized industry will have raised their wages, both groups in the non-unionized industry will have had theirs reduced, and the gains of those remaining in the one will equal the losses of the original and added workers in the other. The total amount received in wages by the body of workers in the two industries will not have altered, but it will be differently distributed between them.

But there are conditions in which the workers employed in both industries taken together could gain, and conditions in which they could lose, if a union successfully raised wages in one of them. If the demand for labour in the unionized industry were inelastic, the rise of rates would lead to a less than proportionate fall in the demand for it, some men would be dislodged, but those remaining in employment would have gained. If the demand in the non-unionized market were elastic, the addition to the number of workers would reduce the wage rate in that market by a smaller percentage, so that though the wages per head there were lower, the aggregate sum received in wages would be greater. There is obviously a degree of inelasticity of demand in the unionized and of elasticity in the competitive labour market such that, though some workers would enjoy a rise and others a fall of wages, the group in the two industries taken as a whole would be better off. For a union or an arbitration tribunal able to foresee and willing to take account of all the facts, there would be an interesting problem of choice of policy! By a similar argument, it could be shown that if the demand for labour in the unionized market were elastic, so that for any given rise of rates a greater percentage of workmen would be displaced, and were inelastic in the competitive market, so that this percentage addition to the working force led to a greater percentage fall of wage rate, there would be a decreased aggregate amount received in wages in both trades, although those still in employment in the unionized industry would have gained.

This example, though simplified, is not therefore fanciful. For not only does it have some likeness to cases where a given type of labour is employed mainly in two industries, but it can easily be adapted to bring in the third market of 'miscellaneous industries' referred to above. This is clear if we think of two unionized industries, say building and shipbuilding, as equal in size to the third, the group of miscellaneous industries where there is no union. The pressure of the displaced workers migrating from the two unionized industries would then be concentrated on the miscellaneous trades, which at the outset provided only a third of the total field of employment, with corresponding effects on the wage rate.

This reasoning can be illustrated by a simplified example using some of the facts contained in the report of the Court of Inquiry into the engineering dispute of 1954. The two largest industrial sub-groups, the engineering and electrical industries, and the vehicle industry, employed 1,260,000 and 663,000 males respectively, but there were also 631,000 engineers employed in a third group of industries, which included shipbuilding, railway loco shops, motor repairing, etc., for which there were separate employers' negotiating organizations. Let us treat these as the three separate labour markets: the first two unionized, the third—shipbuilding and other industries—as if it were non-unionized, and take the average earnings of the time workers at that date, 190s., as the uniform wage prevailing in all three markets. Suppose the demand curve for labour in all three markets is represented by a straight line inclined at an angle of 45°.[1] If the union in the first two markets obtained a rise of about 10 per cent to make the wage 210s., the effect would be to reduce employment in those industries to 1,060,000 and

[1] In diagrams representing these calculations, the scales are such that the distance along the horizontal axis representing 1 million workers is the same as the distance on the vertical axis representing a wage rate of 100s.

463,000, thus dislodging 200,000 workers from each of them. If these 400,000 surplus workers migrated to the non-unionized third market, wages per head there would fall to about 150s., and the aggregate wages paid in that group rise from £5,995,000 to £7,730,000. But though the workers left in the first two markets would now be enjoying another pound a week each, there would be fewer of them and the total wages paid in those two groups of industries would have fallen from £11,970,000 to £11,130,000 and from £6,298,000 to £4,862,000. But the total wages of the whole body of workers in all three markets together would have decreased by £520,000. If, however, the demand curve for labour in all three markets could be represented by a straight line inclined not at 45°, but at 60°, the workers in the two unionized industries would gain substantially. Very few workers would be dislodged from them, so that the pressure on the third, open market would be less than in the previous case and wages would fall by £2, the slightly increased number of workers now employed in it getting a little more in total than before. The total amount of wages in all three markets together would be practically unaltered, but would be differently distributed between the three, the organized having gained at the expense of the unorganized.

Given a little patience, the analysis could obviously be extended to cover more complicated cases of four, five, six or more markets, and by assuming the markets of equal or different sizes and varied elasticities of demand for labour, to indicate the way in which labour would be redistributed between them and by what amount wages in the non-unionized markets would fall below those in the unionized markets.

It seems clear that events such as these must have taken place during the stages of incomplete unionization, when unions were strong only in some industries or some areas. The creation of a union would begin where some identity of interests existed between workmen, such as is provided by common participation in the same industry or by working together in the same or adjacent work places. Miscellaneous industries and outlying districts would be brought into the union field last. Some of the disparities of wages noted in the late nineteenth and early twentieth centuries could no doubt be attributed to some redistribution of labour of this kind between unionized and non-unionized trades. And the relatively low wages in various trades later brought under the Trades Boards and Wages Councils may have been partly due to their position as open, residual, unorganized trades.

7. UNIONS IN ALL TRADES

But suppose *all* industries are unionized? All we need do is to imagine what broadly has happened historically, that the residual, unorganized trades either become unionized or are made the subject of 'substitute' collective bargaining through Wages Councils. Then the number which could be absorbed into the once unorganized industries would be limited by the rate of wages which the collective agreement or wage order prescribed for them, and the final re-distribution of labour would depend on the degree of pressure exerted by unions and the elasticity of demand for labour in each industry. Workers in some industries would gain, relatively, and others lose, relatively, and in this sense wages in the various indus-tries would be 'out of line'. The effect of the activities of the Wages Councils and Wages Boards, including the Agricultural Wages Board, has been to put a 'floor' to wages and to raise it a bit. If all unions pushed their rates up high enough, there could be a dislodged surplus of workers unable to get work anywhere at the current rates. In fact, it is extremely difficult to organize *every* trade: some here and there find odd jobs to do—painting, gardening, personal service, or start modest lines of trading, etc.; and in the inter-war years numbers took up arduous and hazardous jobs as house-to-house canvassers, largely on a commission basis. It is remarkable that during the great depression of the 'thirties, when South Wales was devastated by the collapse of the coal industry, the numbers employed in the consumers' trades, such as retail distribution, restaurants, entertainments and sports, nevertheless increased.

These conclusions are not invalidated because they seem to fly in the face of the current fact, that nearly all-round unionization is combined with full employment. In conditions of economic growth, of expanding markets and of technical change, new products and new services develop, which take to themselves the more lively, more mobile and less encumbered workers with near-by skills, and thus relieve the pressure. All this means is that the realignment of wages due to the redistribution of labour through union pressures may be intermingled with a change in relative wage rates due to expansion and the opening of new opportunities. But the process is taking place all the same.

The limit of a union's power of eating into the payment for the use of capital is the elasticity of supply of it, for though in the short run much of it may be immobile, in the long run the considerable supplies needed for replacement, renewals and expansion can be diverted to the non-unionized or weakly unionized fields. In the formal words of the text-books, capital can move 'elsewhere'. But when all fields are unionized, there is no 'elsewhere' free from some degree of union pressure, and the net reward of capital in general would therefore be decreased. Will the reduction of its price lead to a fall in the total supply of it, i.e. discourage saving and encourage consumption? If it did, the capital available for working with labour would be decreased and aggregate wages might fall. This could occur if the savers' standards of consumption were rigid and tenaciously held, so that they would, if necessary, reduce savings in order to maintain them. But while workers and capitalists alike try vigorously to defend their existing standards against reduction, they are not likely to react so strongly to attempts to prevent them from rising to a level they have never enjoyed. There is thus some element of convention in the amount of saving which takes place in response to a given rate of interest. To taxpayers who in 1909–10 protested against an income tax increased from 1s. to 1s. 2d. and a supertax of 6d., it would have appeared inconceivable that savings should not dry up if the rate were 8s. 6d.; it has not done so because over periods of time new generations appear to whom high tax rates are normal and expected, for they have no practical experience of any other. In the same way, we could get used to a lower reward of capital as a result of all-round union pressure, provided it restrained the rise, rather than demanded a fall of the savers' standards of consumption. The question is whether the net yield of investment is being reduced below the conventional minimum of the time.

8. UNIONS BARGAINING WITH ORGANIZED EMPLOYERS

So far we have assumed that there was competition between employers for workpeople and competition between consumers for the product. If we now take account of the fact that any 'monopolistic' power of the unions may be counterbalanced by the employers' combinations, we shall have a picture, recognizably like much of the contemporary world, of unions bargaining with organized employers acting as 'only' or monopolistic buyers of labour. And such employers' associations may be acting also as monopolists in the sale of their products. There is thus a variety of situations in which a trade union may have to operate and its power to 'maximize' wages, or more strictly, maximize the excess of wages over what they would have been in the absence of a union, varies accordingly. Some of these situations are favourable, others unfavourable to their exercise of such power. For example, amongst situations which a union may have to face are the following:

	Employers		*Consumers*
	as buyers of labour	as sellers of product	
1.	competing	competing	competing
2.	monopoly	competing	competing
3.	monopoly	monopoly	competing
4.	monopoly	monopoly	monopoly

It is clear from inspection that the bargaining strength of the union is least limited in cases of type 1. In type 3 the union's power is balanced by the employer's power as a monopoly buyer of labour; the bargaining between them may shift part of the burden on to the unorganized consumer, since the union may press for high rates which the employers can pay by charging monopolistic prices for a limited output. Case No. 2 is not uncommon, for often employers do associate for the purpose of making wage agreements whilst competing in the sale of their products. But the consumers may also combine: this may happen when they are manufacturers purchasing materials from a previous stage of manufacture, or merchants combining for the purchase of imported materials or products. If a proposal made by Mr. E. F. Wise to the Royal Commission on *Food Prices*[1] that imported meat should be purchased by State boards, acting as only buyer, had been adopted, there would have been, for example, a trade union in New Zealand bargaining with employers and packers; that producer's organization acting as only seller to Britain, whose Import Board acted as only buyer.

[1] Vol. III. App. LXXIII; 1925 Non-Parl.

There is one obvious case of a 'buyer's monopoly' exercising its powers by fixing a maximum wage. This was the agreement of professional football clubs fixing the maximum wages which clubs might give players and which they might not exceed even although the capital value of a player, as assessed by transfer fees, might reach a sum twice that of his pay for the rest of his playing life. The Football League argued that it did not mind what the maximum wage was, so long as it was within the capacity of all clubs, without exception, to pay. Adam Smith's 'tacit agreement' of employers is here an explicit one, made in the interests not of maximizing the profit of the participating clubs, but rather of maintaining the organization of the professional game and the league system as a whole, and enforced by powers of inspection of books and of fines on clubs and players, etc. And in this case there are varying degrees of imperfect competition in the sale of the product or service, since each club is separated from other clubs by distance, and has a core of loyal supporters, even when there are two such clubs in or near the same town. The development of a players' trade union has essentially altered this position.[1]

Some care is needed in interpreting the term 'monopoly buyer of labour'. The strict sense of 'only buyer' would mean not only that the firm or association of firms acting in concert was the only purchaser, but that therefore the specialized workers had no alternative employment, and that if they were non-unionized and competing, would have to accept any rate of pay above dispute pay or unemployment benefit or any private sources they might possess. In such a situation one might suppose that at any wage a little above that minimum the entire available labour supply would seek employment. Such cases are rare, but something resembling them not impossible. A practical case nearly like this theoretical one can be modified and from it a theoretical example constructed to show the possibilities. Before 1914 and the later difficulties in certain localized sections of the lace trade caused by decline of demand, lace twist hands were highly specialized workers, earning wages on the whole exceptional at that time. They could (as the depression in the inter-war years showed) transfer to other occupations only with considerable difficulty and substantial loss of

[1] *Association Football*. Cttee. Rep. pp. 23, 28–30, 47–50; 1952 Non-Parl. Min. of Labour. See also T.U.C., Southport, 1955. Rep. pp. 320–2. *Eastham* v. *Newcastle United F.C.* [1963] 3 ALL E.R.

earnings. Let us suppose there were no openings at all for them. If (pursuing the modification of the facts to make the case resemble the theoretical one more closely) the employers now organized themselves as an only buyer, one could think of a rate of wages a little bit above the minimum provided by benefit or other resources which would give the employers an offer of the entire supply.

The term 'monopoly buyer' is ordinarily used, however, not in this strict sense of 'only buyer' but as meaning 'very large buyer'. What is in mind is the power of one firm which is also an industry to bargain, or a combination of all the firms in an industry who have formerly competed for the labour to bargain collectively. But although the only buyer of labour for that industry, it may not be the only buyer of that class of labour. Indeed, the assumption that a very large buyer of labour wishing to enlarge his labour force must offer a steadily increasing wage to secure them presumes that they are working in other industries from which they can be attracted only at steadily increasing cost. If, therefore, we think of the employers as being organized into the sixteen groups (leaving out the 'non-manual' and 'general workers' groups) into which Trades Union Congress has for its own purposes divided its affiliated unions, there must clearly be a considerable number of them which, even if they acted as monopoly buyers for their own industry would, according to their size, be only 'moderately large' buyers competing for certain classes of labour also employed by other industries. It is therefore wise not to jump too soon in applying monopoly theory to cases where an individual industry is organized as a single buyer.

The same sort of attention to probable facts seems necessary when we ask what would happen if a trade union intervened to make with a very large buyer a collective agreement for a uniform, standard wage. It would be possible to show that since the employer would be buying labour at rising (marginal) wages, a collective agreement for a standard wage at some lower rate would make it profitable for him to increase his labour force—i.e. employment would increase. Unionization would have increased employment. This might be true if the union set out simply to maximize employment, but only on the most unreal assumptions about union's or men's economic behaviour. Is it to be expected that workers would go to the trouble of organizing and paying union officers to make an agreement reducing their own wages below those already offered by the 'large

G

buyer of labour' in order to give employment to additional workers already in work elsewhere?

If we wish to advance from these general propositions to more precise statements about the processes of bargaining between a fully organized union and a fully organized employers' association, it is necessary not to be afraid of being 'very theoretical'. The analysis of a labour market in which both workers and employers are fully competing is easy, since it can be shown that there is some rate of wages at which all the workers will be employed and at which the number of workers the employers will take on and the number who will accept jobs is 'about equal'. Strictly, exactly equal. But since it takes time and money to move from one industry to another and for knowledge of vacancies and of workers seeking jobs to spread through the market, the two quantities in practice are never, except by chance, exactly equal, though the economic calculations of all parties will be continually carrying them towards a rate which would make them so. Many of the employers who gave evidence before the Royal Commission on Trade Unions, even those who were not really well disposed to trade unions, agreed that by spreading knowledge of the supply of and demand for labour amongst their members, the unions had made wage rates more uniform—in this respect, more like a competitive market.[1] They were, of course, performing the functions later taken on by the Employment Exchanges.

But bargaining between a union and an employers' association is more complicated. That there may be elements of bluff in it is plain, since unions often ask for more than they expect to get—even when it is generally well known that they will accept less, and employers' associations make a first refusal when they really intend to make concessions. Nevertheless, it is right to begin by over-rationalizing the bargaining process, in order to see what the behaviour of both parties might be if they were moved solely by precise economic calculation. We need not overstress this in order

[1] *Organization and Rules of Trade Unions and other Associations.* R. Com. 11th Rep. App. Answers to Questions. For example, answers of Cail, p. 99; Holmfirth Chamber of Commerce, p. 89; B. Samuelson, p. 135; J. Smith, p. 137; S. Smith, p. 138; Leslie, p. 118; J. Robinson, p. 131; 1868–69 [4123–I], xxxi. Note also H. M. Thompson's comment: 'Do not the evils which trade unionism has wrought by hampering the action of competition, sink into insignificance by the side of the immense benefits it has brought by *increasing* in other ways effective competition?' *The Theory of Wages.* 1892. p. 118.

to realize that it takes a more prominent place in wage discussions than it did in Galsworthy's *Strife*. In consequence, economists have exercised considerable ingenuity in working out solutions on various assumptions about the way each side could weigh up the issues involved, and in working out illustrative systems of diagrams.[1]

The central question can be put in a form which indicates its practical as well as its theoretical relevance: is there one wage rate, and one only, which could be arrived at by an independent arbitrator who knew fully the interests of both parties, and on which the two groups would agree, or is there only a range of such rates, it being an arbitrary matter at what precise wage within the range a settlement would be made? Arguments have been advanced to show that either result is possible according to the conditions specified. For the present purpose it is sufficient to look at one of the ways in which it can be shown that there is a *range* of wage rates at any one of which a settlement between a union and employers could be made.

The interests of both trade union and employers' association would fix upper and lower limits to the wage rate. There is *some* rate of wages which would so reduce employment that the union would not wish to press beyond it, and its private doubts about it would increase the nearer the wage moved to that point; obviously employers would wish to pay less than this if they could. There is also *some* figure below which the employers would not wish to drive the rate because they would then have difficulty in recruiting or retaining sufficient labour; and the unions would certainly press for a higher one. It is between these two limits that the bargaining will fix the rate. The range between the two may be very narrow, as the cessations of work which occur over very small money differences show. Sometimes it is wide and there is room for a good deal of manoeuvring. For if the demand for labour were inelastic, the workers could push the rate towards the upper limit, while if the supply of it were inelastic, so that a fall in the wage offered did not proportionately discourage recruitment by the industry, the employers would more easily push it downwards. It would obviously be narrow if both demand for it and the supply of it were elastic, since a high rate would choke off demand and a low rate divert the

---

[1] For example, A. C. Pigou. *Principles and Methods of Industrial Peace.* 1905. App. A; F. Zeuthen. *Problems of Monopoly.* 1930. Chap. IV; J. Hicks. *Theory of Wages.* 1963. Chap. VIII; J. T. Dunlop. *Wage Determination under Trade Unions.* 1950. Chap. V.

supply of workers. The range would thus depend on the facts in any given case.

Is this all we can say? No, if we assume that employers work solely on straightforward monetary calculations—as left-wing propagandists say they do—and that the union does the same. Stoppages of work imply that each side has a point above or below which—as the case may be—it will make no further concessions. What these 'sticking points', as Pigou calls them, are can be seen most easily on the employers' side. His accountants can tell him not only how much the increase of wages will cost, but also how much the dispute will cost each day it goes on; he can estimate how much he would gain by obtaining a lower rate of wages, or by not having to pay a higher rate. What he does not know is the length of the strike. Victory depends on a number of factors, of which generalship is one. Sometimes the final outcome seems obvious from the beginning; at others, as in military struggles, there can be surprises, and what appeared to be the strongest side may lose. Where the employers' side consists of one firm or 'unit of financial control', it would be able to get clear ideas on its own staying power, and if because of the nature of its commitments the cost per day varied with the length of the strike, it could know that too. If, on the other hand, the association consisted of financially independent concerns of different sizes and economic strength, each could come to his side's meeting with his sum done, but their 'sticking points' might be different and would have to be reconciled in a common policy. It was common knowledge during the printers' dispute that the losses bore much more severely on some newspapers than on others.

The calculations on the union side are not so straightforward, for it does not receive wages; what a dispute costs it as an organization are not wages lost, but what it gives out as dispute pay. This it can vary if the stoppage is prolonged and as its funds diminish; it can deposit its securities with its bankers as the basis for a loan, etc. But prolonged disputes can sometimes run on very little. No one who witnessed the distribution of a pathetic 6d. a week to which some of the miners' districts were reduced during the prolonged strike of 1926, for all its encouragement of courage and endurance of suffering, could imagine that this mite really affected the length of the dispute. No doubt if the men are on time rates or have been drawing not too dissimilar earnings, with piece and overtime rates, a calculation could be made of the weekly loss of wages of the members concerned, and it is clear from the figures occasionally stated when a dispute is over that now and again somebody does this kind of sum.[1] The critical point is the strain on the individual members involved, and thus turns on the differences between earnings and whatever the dispute pay is. And although the matter will be complicated by varied personal circumstances regarding family commitments, hire purchase and building society payments, etc., it is not hard for a union's officers to have a common-sense knowledge of how much members' savings and other resources are being eaten into, and 'how long they can last'. Members of co-operative societies can pile up debts against the sums in their name, or obtain further credit. There may be help from other unions if the dispute is one of an important principle: during 1926 the miners received substantial help from other unions, etc. In some districts the Board of Guardians gave out-relief to families on a considerable scale, not, apparently, always legally.[2] Indeed, without resources of this kind it is difficult to see how a very long dispute could be endured. About 86 per cent of Northumberland and Durham miners applied for relief for their families during the dispute.[3] Under the National Assistance Act, 1948, if they are in need a striker's dependents have to be provided for in the same way as other applicants. In 1955, 18,660 out of 235,000 workpeople involved in disputes with which the Board were concerned received £155,580.[4]

[1] Cost of Manchester (Salford) Dock Strike: loss of wages, £150,000; of traffic receipts, £100,000; 1950–51 Cmd. 8375, xvi.

[2] *Chester-le-Street Union.* Report on the Administration; 1927 Cmd. 2818, xi. The Guardians 'appointed to take over the administration expressed the view that the public funds had been used for the benefit of a Trade Union engaged in a dispute'.

[3] H. F. Hohman. *The Development of Social Insurance and Minimum Wage Legislation in Great Britain.* 1933. p. 347. Note 2. pp. 308–9; pp. 340–7, has a useful account of the whole problem at that date. The author notes that during the strike of 1920, no concerted action was taken to get relief for strikers' families.

[4] *National Assistance Board.* Rep., 1955. p. 12; 1955–56 Cmd. 9781, xi. Rep., 1954. p. 11; 1955–56 Cmd. 9530, xi. The person striking cannot get assistance for his own requirements, unless he is in urgent need, but dependents must be provided for on the same conditions as other applicants. The dependents would not be regarded as in need so long as they had resources, including strike pay, deferred wages and income-tax refunds sufficient for their needs on the assistance scale. In 1954 the scale rate was 89s. 6d. for man, wife, one child 5–11 and one under 5.

The weighing of costs and gains would be decisive in determining union and employers' policy if they 'shunned all violence of rage, passion and humour', as they are sometimes urged to do, and concentrated entirely on economic calculation; this somewhat over-rationalized account would then represent what takes place. But in practice some qualifications have to be made. First, neither party knows the actual gains or actual costs until the agreement is finally made, so that what they have to compare is expected costs and expected gains and each may make wrong forecasts of these, either from lack or inaccurate knowledge of market facts or from lack of knowledge of the mind of the other party. Then the fact that there is a range of wage rates at any one of which agreement is possible and that each sides' knowledge of the other's mind is imperfect, opens the way and gives a valid excuse for bluff, for keeping in the background information about what would be at a pinch acceptable, for pitching initial claims high (or low) so that acceptance of lower (or higher) figures, wears an air of concession, and for other devices aimed at influencing the mind of the other party.[1] It is part of a labour conciliation officer's job, when his services are made use of, to meet the two parties separately and thus find out some of the things in each party's mind which they are not willing (at that stage) to reveal to one another. It is such knowledge which may enable him to find an 'acceptable formula' which they cannot find for themselves.

Unless the union can impose a condition about the numbers to be employed ('there must be no redundancy') the volume of employment which results from the bargaining will depend on what price is eventually fixed for the product. For although it is common to speak of a union as 'sharing the spoils with a monopoly', the wage increase does not, as a tax could, take the form of a percentage of monopoly profit, but is a rise in costs, a shift of the cost curve. And the employers' side, in fact, usually consists not of a strict, single firm monopoly, but of a group of financially autonomous firms, negotiating as a unit on the rates of wages to be paid by its members, some of whom will be strong and efficient, while others will be weaker or even 'no-profit' firms. Much depends, therefore, on the success of the employers' group in getting a rate which its

[1] For a purely theoretical discussion of the point, see G. S. Shackle. *The Nature of the Bargaining Process.* In, J. T. Dunlop (ed.). *The Theory of Wage Determination.* 1957.

weaker 'marginal' members can pay without contracting their output,[1] or on how far that output can, by competition or agreement, be taken over by the stronger. Where, as might be the case in a multi-product industry such as 'engineering', there are a number of single firms, or groups of two or three firms making specialized products with little markets of their own, the effect of a uniform wage rate on the prices of the separate products would vary with the percentage which labour costs formed of total costs. The relative prices and output of these products and the balance of employment between the sub-industries would correspondingly alter. A variety of other factors, such as changes in other costs, and changes in the demands for the different products, would be operating at the same time, but though obscured and even overweighted, the rise of labour cost would be making its contribution to the final result.

9. MATTERS NOT CONNECTED WITH THE AMOUNT OF THE WAGE

Unions are not concerned solely with maximizing wages, for there are other matters to which they may sometimes attach as much or even greater importance, and from this arise many practices and disputes which at first sight seem to be aside from the main issue or even trivial. The most obvious are the rights of the union itself, including 'recognition'. Though there are still non-unionized areas, in principle and in practice this battle has been largely won, but to win it unions have not uncommonly terminated a strike by sacrificing the whole or part of a wage claim in order to secure something of more importance—recognition. This may include such buttressing rights as that of electing persons of their own choice to check outputs on which wages are calculated, such as miner's checkweighmen, or the replacement of the repulsive system of using employer's foremen for selecting dockers for calls to work. Then often members have been urged not to 'weaken the union' and therefore to return to work (if the stoppage is unofficial), not to return to work (until negotiations have been completed), not to countenance dissident movements or breakaway unions, but to honour agreements or follow agreed procedure, or to accept compromise terms obtained.

[1] 'It is no secret that even in many industries for which basic wages are negotiated nationally there are many individual employers who are in a position to meet the unions' demands much more generously but who allow the less efficient firms to influence settlements unduly.' Alan Birch. 'Through a Trade Unionist's Eyes.' *The Times*. Jan. 31st, 1958. p. 9f.

The union thus has a life of its own as distinct from that of its individual members, so that its preservation may sometimes be called for even at the expense of sacrificing an immediate wage claim. Secondly, where there are rival or competing unions, the wage demands each makes may be influenced by its desire to maintain its position against that of its rival. The successive wage claims of the N.U.R. and the A.S.L.E.F. have clearly had in them an element of competitive leapfrogging; the independent strike of loco men which achieved a rise of 3s. only was counted as a justified endeavour to maintain the skilled man's differentials. In such conditions a union must achieve some minimum if it is to retain its members.

Thirdly, the arrangements of the labour market are not always of the simple employer-employed type based on an employment contract terminable at a week's or fortnight's notice, but may be hedged about by property rights in the job itself. Thus by tradition the sons of certain classes of port workers have prior claims on jobs in that trade; recruitment is not free. Then in the London docks there is an understanding that ships of some lines should be handled by stevedores, while the others 'belong' to dockers.[1] A strike occurred in an inter-union dispute because a change in the ownership of the *Daily Sketch*, up till then printed in a works customarily regarded as the preserve of the members of the Printing Machine Managers' Trade Society, an old-established craft union with apprenticeship rules, involved its being printed in another works which 'belonged' to NATSOPA, which had none.[2] The difficulties of organizing insurance companies' employees have arisen partly from the peculiarities of the trade. Some of them 'purchase a book', somewhat as a business man might purchase a milk or newspaper round, have property rights in it and earn commission, while others do not, and are employed on an ordinary wage basis.

Fourthly, something of the same conception of property in the job, allied with fears of unemployment, shows itself in the area still in some measure disputed with management, of rights in the selection of persons to be dismissed as redundant—whether it should be on the basis of 'last in, first out', whether shop stewards should or

---

[1] *Unofficial Stoppages in the London Docks.* Cttee. Rep. p. 23; 1950–51 Cmd. 8236, xvi.

[2] *NATSOPA, the Printing Machine Managers' Trade Soc., etc. Dispute.* Ct. of Inquiry. Rep.; 1952–53 Cmd. 8931, xiii.

should not be subject to this or any other common rule;[1] whether and to what extent unions should be consulted, what notice and compensation if any should be paid. The Amalgamated Engineering Union in 1956 resolved on an out and out resistance to redundancy, but after a point it may clearly be impracticable to hold to this position. The Confederation of Shipbuilding and Engineering Unions has discussed a policy involving the right of prior notification and consultations, considerations of length of service in the firm, priority in re-engagement and local negotiations since prosperous firms may be able to offer better terms than struggling ones.

10. Wage Awards: on what Principles are they based?

We now turn to examine the principles which have been invoked in the settlement of wage claims. To discover these we have to draw mainly on the reports and findings of the Committees and Courts, for when claims are settled by direct negotiation in private, formal statements of reasons are unnecessary, the task of the negotiating representatives of each side being rather to explain to their respective members what had been achieved and why this or that concession had to be made to secure agreement. And those explanations may be concerned as much with the tactics of bargaining as with any economic principles involved in the terms of settlement. But we know from speeches and published reports that the economic reasoning used by either side is not very different from that presented in hearings before Committees and Courts; what is then put forward is often only the final version of what had been argued at earlier stages.

It would be idle to expect a settled and consistent body of principles of wage fixing to emerge from these findings and awards. Those who look to them for broad principles on which to reconstruct the wage and salary structure of the country will be disappointed, for the best of reasons: these bodies are not called upon to decide whether film stars should be paid more than shop girls, or doctors more than dockers, but to adjudicate on particular disputes about the amount by which an existing wage or salary, high or low, should be somewhat increased or decreased. Apart, possibly, from a few special cases, both the claims by the unions

[1] *Austin Motor Co. Ltd. and ... the National Union of Vehicle Builders. Dispute.* Ct. of Inquiry. Rep. paras. 28, 73; 1952–53 Cmd. 8839, xiii.

and the awards made assume the broad relationships between the various grades of employment as they are found in the market. Nor, since the findings and awards are made for separate industries at different times and in different conditions of trade and prosperity, should one expect to find too much consistency in the principles applied; indeed, for these very reasons there is a sense in which they ought not to be consistent. Over a period of time claimants may urge and tribunals accept first one, then another, even contrary argument. At one time it may be 'under-manning', at another a 'rise in productivity', at a third a 'failure of wages to keep pace with those in comparable industries', but on each occasion these *may* be correct descriptions of the current market situation. A rise in demand which in the earlier competitive or, more strictly, non-unionized labour market was followed by marginal wage increases here and there spreading, stickily perhaps, until the whole level altered, in a unionized world results in a negotiated wage rise at a given date for the entire market. The unspoken, 'automatic' and impersonal 'causes' of the old non-unionized markets may thus become spoken arguments formally advanced by the union and employers' negotiators.

Then the economic arguments set forth by the disputants are not exercises in discovering impartially the most relevant economic principles, but statements of a case. Indeed, sometimes the economic reasoning used—on both sides—would be sorrowfully awarded very low marks in an examination; the case, or parts of the case, the spokesmen are instructed to present is sometimes thin, and they have to do the best they can to buttress it. The nearest example of a scientific investigation was that of the Samuel Commission on the *Coal Industry* (*1925*) which, though its terms of reference were made wide in order to meet the view of the miners that the organization of the industry was in question, really arose from the demand of the owners that wages should be reduced and hours of work lengthened and the insistence of the miners that they would accept neither. The Commissioners were able men of great experience and known driving capacity, and they were aided by the knowledge and resources for investigation possessed by Government Departments as well as by the industry. They were able, amongst other things, to range firms into groups according to costs, to estimate the proportion of output produced at a loss and the addition to unemployment which certain proposals would involve.

Two other bodies, the Oaksey Committee on the *Police Conditions of Service*[1] and the Working Party on the *Recruitment and Training of Nurses*,[2] were both able to get full details of the numbers in the services, the authorized establishment or requirement, the wastage rate and so the annual intake of recruits required. But those were easy cases, since the services are not commercial products sold at some price which affects demand and employment figures. Inquiries on this scale are not normally either possible or necessary in Court or Tribunal cases, which concern disputes in industries in a normal, not a critical condition, and the six months which even the fast-driven Samuel Commission took would be intolerable in an ordinary dispute. The inquiries into the shipbuilding and engineering disputes of 1957 each took three weeks.

(a) Early principles. (i) Wages to attract labour

Two different sets of principles emerged early in the century when the wages of two distinct groups came up for decision. The first consisted of certain State servants in regular employment—the Irish police, postal workers and teachers, to each of whose cases was applied the final overriding principle that the pay should be such as to attract and retain a sufficient number of entrants. The claim of the Royal Irish Constabulary in 1902 that pay should be increased because it was lower than that of forces in England, was rejected on the ground that it was a rural force which could not be put on a par with those of English towns, that although basic pay was below that of artisans, with the value of the pension it exceeded that of the majority of them, and that there were many applications for vacancies and few resignations. But by 1914 the number of applications was much smaller than the number of vacancies, and by 1920 the scales were to 'harmonize' with those for Great Britain.[3] In 1904 the Bradford Committee on *Post Office Wages* put aside comparisons with outside industry: the State should determine its policy irrespective of what others might do, neither following an example nor setting one. The test was whether the wages were adequate to secure the requisite number of applicants, whether these on trial proved to have the proper capacity and whether the pay

[1] Rep. Pts. I and II; 1948–49 Cmd. 7674, Cmd. 7831, xix.
[2] Rep.; 1947 Non-Parl. Min. of Health.
[3] Rep.; 1904 Cd. 2170, xxxiii; also *Breviate, 1900–1916*. p. 217.

was likely to secure the contentment and hearty response of the staff.
They were found to be adequate on the first two counts, but not on
the third. The Stephen Committees of 1918 on the salaries of
teachers in elementary and in secondary schools concluded that
although women teachers' work was similar to and as zealously
performed as that of men teachers, their salaries should be lower
because a salary which would attract sufficient women would not
be adequate to attract sufficient men.[1] The Anderson Committee
on the *Pay of State Servants* (*1923*) concluded that there was 'only
one principle in which all the factors of responsibility, cost of living,
marriage, children, social position, etc., are included—an employer
should pay what is necessary to recruit and retain an efficient staff'.

(ii) *Living wages, fair wages, what the traffic will bear*

But in the sweated trades, whose wages the Trades Boards were
to raise because they were 'unduly low', the problem was not one of
attracting workers, for some of the difficulties were due to the fact
that there was a surplus of them, but of deciding on what principles
the new higher wage rates should be fixed. The Boards were, in
England, an experiment, and the early ones proceeded fairly
cautiously by moving upwards from existing rates. No guidance
was given in the Act and the three principles which emerged were
'a living wage', 'a fair wage' and 'a wage that the traffic would bear'.
Which of these principles should be given primacy? The Boards
seem to have been guided by a mixture of all three, some emphasiz-
ing one more than the others, but none of them apparently allowing
the first two to override the third. The English Boards did not, as
did Australian Courts, undertake detailed investigation as to what
a living wage was; some members, indeed, holding that if Parliament
had intended a uniform basis of that kind for all the trades concerned, it would not have established separate Boards. They thus
had in mind a vague sort of standard, but once having expressed it in
terms of specific rates, did in fact try to keep it constant in real
terms by adjusting the rates for changes in the cost of living. This
empirical attitude, apparently unenterprising intellectually, had its
practical advantages, for it did not involve the somewhat futile task
of defining precisely what was meant, whether it was to be a physio-
logical minimum, a subsistence wage or to include elements of the

[1] *Construction of Scales of Salary for Teachers in Elementary Schools.* Dept.
Cttee. Rep.; 1917–18 Cd. 8939, xi; also *Breviate, 1917–1939.* p. 485.

'psychological standard' implied in the 'natural wage' as conceived by Torrens and Ricardo; and it avoided the egregious result which followed Australian calculations based on the needs of a man and wife and three children, that industry was asked to pay for 450,000 non-existent wives and 2,000,000 non-existent children.[1] Fair wages—usually taken to mean, in Marshall's words, wages similar to those in trades involving equal difficulty and disagreeableness, and requiring equal natural abilities and expensiveness of training— imply definitions of skill, and the comparison and assessment of diverse types of jobs; for equalizing wages which were not fair in the sense defined implied that unequal wages had to be given where the degree of skill was different. This involved comparisons with the wages received by relevant skill in other trades, and presently the argument began to slide into the question whether they were enough to attract a sufficient supply of skill to the trade.

The principle of what the trade could bear was in effect raised by the Committee on *Home Work*, 1908,[2] when it found that wages were low in some of the sweated trades because if the prices of the goods, e.g. women's clothing, were higher, customers could easily make the articles for themselves. In effect, the Committee held that the principle of the living wage should be enforced even if the trade could not bear it, for it declared that an industry which could not pay its workers a minimum income 'should not continue'. But if those dislodged from employment were marginal, not very efficient workers unable easily to get a footing in any industry, and no employment could be found for them, as we have seen on p. 52 above, the rise of pay might not increase and could decrease the total sum paid in wages. At the establishment of Boards there was usually a great variety of rates of pay in each industry, some big, efficient firms paying substantially more than less efficient ones. The Boards in general refused to accept the plea, just as trade unions have always done in direct bargaining, that rates should be based on those which could be afforded by the least efficient employer only just able to carry on: on the contrary, it has been those paid by the 'reputable' firms they have tended to select to set the pace. It follows that the task, whether consciously so regarded or not, was one of deciding which was the marginal firm, and what

[1] H. Heaton. *Modern Economic History*. 1921. p. 189.
[2] *Breviate, 1900–1916*. p. 211.

proportion of the firms was to be squeezed out: in fact, what size the industry was to be.[1]

These considerations appear again in the cases presented to the existing Courts and Tribunals. Wages of skilled men are said to be 'deplorable'; family budgets may be presented; wages are said to be unfair as compared with those of other crafts or other industries; industries are said to be undermanned and able to bear higher wages. But through the extension of trade unionism, wage regulation and the wide use of the Courts and Tribunals, the principles have been applied to a much wider range of more complicated industries and grades of skill, and have been elaborated, modified and supplemented accordingly. Some of these principles are put forward simultaneously as the basis of a claim: e.g. the cost of living, a reasonable standard, wages below that of comparable industries and the prosperity of the industry.

The generally accepted principle that wages should be adjusted to the cost of living, i.e. that real wages should not fall, needs but brief mention. The practice of linking wages settlements with the cost of living index may be said to have begun in November 1917, when the National Union of Railwaymen agreed that any fresh claim should depend on a given rise in the index.[2]

Though the index was meant to give only a broad average measure of changes in the cost of buying defined basic elements of a frugal working-class standard and not that of any particular grade of worker, it seemed to offer so useful a means of disentangling what was needed to maintain, as distinct from improving, real standards, that it became common practice to include in collective agreements arrangements for automatic increases of pay for every rise of so many points in the index. Industrial friction due to changes in living costs has thus been greatly reduced, but not eliminated. By somewhat disingenuous choice of the basic dates from which to calculate changes, both unions and employers have produced divergent results to support their case;[3] and unions have been led to place as much of the burden of their wage claims on the cost of living index as possible. They have therefore been led to criticize it, often just because it has not shown a rise as great as they wanted

---

[1] E. M. Burns. *Wages and the State*. 1926. Chap. XVI.

[2] G. W. Alcock. *Fifty Years of Railway Trade Unionism*. 1922. p. 507.

[3] For example, in the 1956 engineering dispute. Ct. of Inquiry. Rep. para. 27 ii, 28 iv; 1956–57 Cmnd. 159, xiv.

to claim, sometimes because the rise in price of the elements in it which are bought out of the wife's housekeeping money is greater than that of the other elements bought by the man, who has doubt-less been reminded of the fact.[1] There is thus a good deal of sparring between unions and employers on the matter: if food prices rise more than the index figure, unions argue that in order to protect the lower-paid workers, wages should also rise more, while if the other elements the man buys go up more than the index, then he feels he is getting less than he should.[2] Notwithstanding these difficulties, the general acceptance of the principle that real standards should not be reduced save for gravest reasons will ensure the continued use of some such device. It is obvious, however, that if an industry were declining through fall of demand, insistence on constant real wages would hasten contraction.

(b) Later principles. (i) 'On their merits'

Before examining the interpretation given and relative importance attached to these principles, one matter concerning the presentation of the claims needs to be considered; the 'universe of discourse'. Why should not each claim be dealt with 'on its merits'? This has been urged on occasions by both employers and employed, and nearly always means that one of the parties wishes some matters to be excluded from consideration, though there is naturally no agreement on what these are. As we have seen, the Bradford Committee on the Wages of Postal Workers wished the State to settle its wages independently, 'neither setting an example nor following one'. The Transport Commission wished the N.U.R. claim to be considered 'on its merits', no doubt because the union based its claim partly on wage rates in other industries.[3] The various tribunals themselves have to be wary of importing into their decisions principles too general in character. It is certainly of note that wage-determining tribunals should be criticized for giving in-sufficient attention to the 'merits of the case' and of having a 'wage

[1] *Engineering and Allied Employers' National Federation and ... the Con-federation of Shipbuilding and Engineering Unions. Dispute.* Ct. of Inquiry. Rep. para. 54; 1953–54 Cmd. 9084, xv.

[2] It would appear from a study by Professor R. G. D. Allen that the retail prices index has so far proved a reasonably accurate measure of changes in the cost of living of most grades of wage earners. See, *Economica*, Feb. 1958.

[3] *British Transport Com. and the N.U.R. Dispute.* Ct. of Inquiry. Final Rep, para. 18; 1954–55 Cmd. 9372, v.

policy'[1] and, still more remarkable, that a disappointed trade union officer should charge the Industrial Disputes Tribunal with not dealing with a claim 'purely on its merits', but with having regard to the national economic position.[2] Then when in 1958 the Minister of Labour declined to appoint a committee of inquiry into the London busmen's claim, but was willing to establish one to inquire into the industry as a whole, including, therefore, the position of provincial busmen, the union protested that instead of arranging to deal with the claim 'on its merits', he was dragging in other concerns not parties to the dispute. In a sense this was correct, since the ability of the London Transport Executive to pay increased wages out of its proceeds had nothing to do with the ability of the provincial bus undertakings to pay wages out of their proceeds; but the union's own members had earlier linked the two by declaring a strike with the avowed intention of diminishing the differential rates between London and the provinces, which a new award raising pay in London would again upset. To the provincial busmen the 'merits of the case' had a different meaning.

The demand that claims should be treated on their merits really assumes that industries can be considered in isolation, though, in fact, a recurring theme in unions' post-war claims is that the members' pay is below that of comparable industries. But an industry may draw labour from a class of workmen also drawn upon by some other industry, so that a demand in the one must affect and raise the value of that class of labour in the second. An enlarged demand for bricklayers in the building industry proper can scarcely fail to affect the wages of bricklayers employed in engineering, steel or other 'industries' in which they may be employed. In competitive conditions, the rise of pay in an expanding industry is indeed a signal to those in other industries to think of transferring their services. It was thus relevant for the Committees on Irish Police and the Desborough and Oaksey Committees on British Police to make comparisons with wages in other occupations in a consideration, not of their ethical fairness, but their adequacy for getting the number of recruits required. And a plea that local government officers paid out of local rates should have their case treated 'on its

[1] B. C. Roberts. *Trade Union Behaviour*. In, J. T. Dunlop. *The Theory of Wage Determination*.

[2] *The Times*. Jan. 16th, 1958. p. 10b.

merits', detached from comparisons with other employment, could scarcely have been made in the inter-war years of depression, when bad trade and burdens of unemployment were imperilling the financial stability of some badly hit towns. The Industrial Court itself had argued, in Award 1325, 1927, that the broad principle which should be followed in determining the wages of Post Office servants was that of the maintenance of a 'fair relativity' as between their wages and those in outside industries as a whole.[1]

(ii) *Prosperity and productivity*

In application, the principle of 'what the traffic will bear' has had to be elaborated since the early Trades Boards bore it in mind in their first experiments in wage-fixing. For, as we have seen, the Committee on *Home Work* was apparently willing to envisage, if necessary, a contraction of employment, and it was theoretically possible, up to a point, to increase the aggregate sum received in wages at the same time. This perhaps could be regarded as the meaning of 'the most the traffic can bear'. But the early caution of the Boards, the experience with the dressmaking trades and the problem of the miners' wage policy in the inter-war years showed that the practical issue was what the safety margin should be within the limit of the 'most'.

Where the industry is a competitive one as regards the sale of its products (even though the firms collectively negotiated wage rates) a full inquiry could pick out roughly the firms which a wage increase would put below the new margin; but a monopoly has means of recoupment in prices, and the problem is the more difficult. The requirement that the Transport Commission running the national-ized railways should one year with another cover its costs led the Court of Inquiry to say that where the employer is bound to keep his business going and can neither show a working profit, nor shift the scene of his operations, nor reorganize his capital structure, nor be wound up by his creditors, then the factors which are understood by all as affecting wage rates in normal industry are absent. The conditions in his business are, commercially speaking, artificial, and it therefore becomes necessary to fall back on the expedient of relating wages he should pay to those paid in such comparable

[1] *Civil Service.* R. Com. Rep. p. 82; 1930–31 Cmd. 3909, x, also *Breviate, 1917–1939.* p. 36.

H

industries as may be found.[1] But this makes the position look more rigid than it really is, since the Transport Commission can reduce the size of the industry, whether railways or buses, by cutting off uneconomic services or by raising fares so that marginal consumers decide not to use them. In dealing with the railways unions' pay claim in April 1958, the majority of the Railway Staff National Tribunal declared that accepting it would in a short time raise the deficit above the £250 million allowed to the Transport Commission to unmanageable proportions, and that raising rates and fares would end in the cutting of services. The minority member, however, swept aside the test of ability to pay and 'purely commercial' considerations, making the remarkable statement that the terms of reference did not make the Tribunal competent to say how the Transport Commission should raise the finance necessary to meet the claim. But whatever may be said about the argument for equal pay for equally arduous work, it would scarcely be possible thus to brush aside capacity to pay and the effect on marginal firms and employment in some equally vital private industry. The request for a subsidy for a nationalized industry simply because it is nationalized, in which wages may be higher than in some industries not nationalized, thus ceases to be a purely economic and becomes partly a political question. And the argument that a higher wage is needed for recruiting is weakened to the extent that it should not be necessary to pay higher wages to get men to run uneconomic, losing services.

In the age of post-war inflation, 'what the traffic will bear' becomes 'ability to pay on account of prosperity', and the safety margin turns into 'prudence' in estimating how long prosperity will continue. The Court of Inquiry into the shipbuilding dispute in 1954 regarded cancellations and falling off of new orders as a warning 'it would be imprudent to ignore', while that of 1957, though regarding the immediate prospects as bright, felt that 'it would be imprudent to dispense with caution entirely, as the future rate of growth might not be as great as in the past and that competition might be more severe.[2]

[1] *British Transport Com. and the N.U.R. Dispute.* Ct. of Inquiry. Final Rep. para. 62; 1954–55 Cmd. 9372, v.

[2] *Shipbuilding Employers' Federation and . . . the Confederation of Shipbuilding and Engineering Unions. Dispute.* Ct. of Inquiry. Rep. paras. 38, 39; 1956–57 Cmnd. 160, xiv.

These difficulties have sometimes been met by recognizing that the industry concerned consists of a number of non-competitive undertakings, or sub-industries, and laying down separate wage scales for each of them. The practice which developed during the inter-war years of grading towns, gas, electricity and municipal tramways into groups according to size, output, traffic, etc., and assigning to each group its own wage rates, was based on the assumptions that these factors reflected their costs and financial strength and so determined their ability to pay, and that since the service undertakings could not compete in one another's territory, they could not undercut one another. That the trades served different markets was put forward by a Scottish bobbin and shuttle-making trade as invalidating comparisons with English rates.[1] But though the report of the Court of Inquiry into the engineering dispute of 1954 listed twenty-six different 'industries', mostly with widely different non-competitive markets, e.g. marine engineering, agricultural engineering, electrical machinery, motor vehicles, aircraft, railway carriage and wagons, watches and clocks, and though it is clearly possible that these might be enjoying different degrees of prosperity so that some industries could afford higher wages than others, and the unions had members employed in all of them, neither employers nor unions argued their case on any other basis than 'engineering' as a whole.

(iii) *Reasonable wages*

The principle of the living wage in its present applications need not detain us. Since poverty in the sense of insufficient income for adequate diet in calories and vitamins, and minimal clothing is now of small proportions, claims for a living wage in that sense have faded out of Court arguments. It is now thought of in two forms. First, in those industries where there are piece rates, various bonuses, etc., earnings may differ markedly from basic rates, and the union may argue that the proportion of men on the minimum basic rates is high enough to justify an increase in basic rates to ensure a satisfactory standard of living. Thus, in the engineering trades, in June 1956, under 3 per cent of the fitters were receiving minimum district rates only, and slightly over 5 per cent were earning less than

[1] M. T. Rankin. *Arbitration Principles and the Industrial Court: an analysis of Decisions, 1919–1929.* 1931. p. 66.

10*s*. above the district rate; nearly 15 per cent of the labourers were on minimum rates.[1] But there is usually a certain amount of statistical sparring between the two sides as to what is and what is not the precise figure. Secondly, the 'living wage' has, in statements of claim, tended to become a 'reasonable living standard'. This is sometimes justified by the production of family budgets, and in spite of the Australian calculations of nearly forty years ago and the British Family Census, the tradition of wife and three children dies hard. But the chief argument about reasonableness is now comparison with other industries: and it thus merges into the third principle, the 'fair' wage.

(iv) *Fair Differentials*

During World War II and for some years after it, trade union opinion was reconciled to a narrowing of the differences between the wages of the skilled and of the unskilled: it tallied with their social philosophy at the time. But it was also a natural consequence of full employment. The surplus of unemployed and under-employed unskilled labour—a phenomenon which was central to the whole problem of poverty as the Minority Commissioners on the Poor Law, 1909, saw it—had as its accompaniment low wages, so that the relative rise of pay compared with that of more skilled persons is a sign of social health. But later post-war years have brought both a sharpened awareness of the 'differentials' and a good deal of mutual eyeing by various unions and industries of one another's progress in standards. When instead of wage rises being spread through the system by marginal variations they take place in a whole industry at a given date, and the various national agreements expire and have to be renewed at different times, when inflation is going on steadily during the period and the successive rises are announced in the newspaper headlines and are broadcast on the wireless, this is little to be wondered at. It needs but the addition of a stiff dose of high-pressure selling of consumer's goods to add zest to this competition in standards. The atmosphere so created could not fail to affect those who live in it. The miners' leaders have on occasion frankly said that it was their intention to see that the miners' lowly position in the country's wage structure during the inter-war years should be transformed into the 'best';

[1] Ct. of Inquiry. Rep. para. 41; 1956–57 Cmnd. 159, xiv.

other unions also have claimed that their agreement was the 'best'. And railwaymen and the workers' side of the Council for the distributive trades have both asserted that their wages have not kept pace with those in manufacturing industries.[1] The problem of 'differentials', whether between different degrees of skill, between different industries or between different localities—between 'neighbouring' wage rates in all three senses—has sometimes been given more importance by unions than their own rate of progress. Not the least remarkable feature of this movement is the combination of great sensitivity about some differentials with an apparent acceptance of others which no one seems to worry about.

First, there are claims by unions that wages should be similar 'in comparable industries'. Several particularly notable cases show what the implications are. In 1954 the Court of Inquiry into the provincial bus dispute decided that although they could see no reason for increasing an advance already given, a further increase should nevertheless be granted to make wages comparable with other sections of the transport industry.[2] In the same year the N.U.R. also pressed a claim on the ground that their wages had fallen below those of other industries, average railway earnings of 182s. 10d. comparing unfavourably with 193s. 1d. in building and contracting, 190s. 1d. in mining and quarrying (other than coal) and 205s. 2d. in manufacturing industries, all for somewhat shorter working weeks. Postmen (on whose favourable earnings other industries also had an eye) had starting rates of 152s. rising to 166s. in two years, with a non-contributory pension, as compared with many railwaymen's starting rate of 125s., which might rise to 162s. after many years. It even argued that the advantage of security which railwaymen had enjoyed had been removed by conditions of full employment. The Transport Commission's reply was to quote the average earnings in the provincial tram and bus services of 178s. 4d., and of 186s. in goods transport by road (other than British Road Services).[3] In a remarkable interim report, the Court argued that since the nationalization of railways meant that they were a public utility of first importance, a railwayman should

---

[1] For example, *The Times*. Jan. 2nd, 1958. p. 3c.

[2] *National Council for the Omnibus Industry. Dispute.* Ct. of Inquiry. Rep. para. 67; 1953–54 Cmd. 9093, xv.

[3] *British Transport Com. and the N.U.R. Dispute.* Ct. of Inquiry. Final Rep. paras. 27, 28, 37; 1954–55 Cmd. 9372, v.

receive a fair and adequate wage, which meant that he should be in no worse case than his colleague in a comparable industry.[1] In its final report, issued seventeen days later, the Court added that a fair wage should be no lower and no higher than it should be; and this appeared to be, wages paid 'in such comparable industries as could be found'.[2] But the N.U.R. and the Transport Commission had both named what they regarded as 'comparable industries', and these surely deserved scrutiny. As Lady Williams has properly asked,[3] who is the railwayman's colleague in a comparable industry? Is it in South Wales or Durham the miner, or in villages and country towns the agricultural worker? Industries are made up of the most varied mixtures of different grades of skill, some having a large proportion of craftsmen of different types, others a much lower proportion and therefore a higher proportion of labourers and semi-skilled men. In two industries similar crafts may be paid equal wages, but average wages may be higher in one of them simply because its technical set-up requires the use of a higher proportion of skilled men. The statistically proper comparison is not between industries, but crafts and grades.[4]

Comparable in the sense of 'fair' wages easily turns into comparable in the sense of 'sufficient to compete with other industries drawing on the same class of labour'. This, perhaps, is really the basis of the firemen's persistence in claiming 'parity' with the police. It is a different and sometimes inconsistent principle. The Court accepted the Transport Commission's view that it had to compete and therefore pay rates comparable with those of other industries in order to get suitable staff. But as the Transport Commission claimed that it had reduced its staff from 630,000 in 1947 to 583,000

[1] Rep. para. 10; 1954–55 Cmd. 9352, v.

[2] Rep. paras. 61, 62; 1954–55 Cmd. 9372, v.

[3] Lady G. Williams. 'The Myth of Fair Wages.' *Economic Journal*. Dec. 1956. p. 629.

[4] Comparisons of average earnings of different industries may be misleading not only for this reason, but because in many British industries the addition to basic rates of payments for specially heavy or dirty work, for piece-work or overtime, etc., may make earnings half as much again or even double basic rates. Each side tends to quote basic rates or earnings, whichever suits its book at the moment. Too little is known about the facts and much misleading and wearisome argument could be cut short if we knew for the great industries the numbers employed at different rates of earnings, say in 5s. groups, quartiles, etc., as set out in the great *Earnings and Hours Inquiries* of *1909–13*. A repetition of these inquiries by modern methods is greatly needed.

in 1954, and that in the first six months of the latter year total intake equalled the wastage, and both sides were at some pains rather to deny that the railways were heavily overstaffed, on this test they seem to have been at least roughly 'comparable'. Industries do not, however, compete with one another for labour as a whole, but for different numbers of the various grades of labour. We have seen that the Anderson Committee of 1923 argued that the one test of state servants' pay was their adequacy for recruiting sufficient numbers of suitable staff. The Industrial Court in 1927 expressed the view that the principle was that of 'a maintenance of fair relativity as between their wages and those in outside industries as a whole, and as between the various classes within the postal service . . .'. The Controller of the Establishments Department of the Treasury interpreted the principle that pay should be adequate to secure the recruitment of a fully qualified staff as meaning that pay and conditions must compare well with those normally available outside the public service in competing occupations. But this, precisely interpreted, is not 'fair relativity' at all, but the test of market value. For the demand for one particular craft or grade of skill and therefore its market price might increase; and then the customary 'skill' differential of the various classes within the service would be upset. The conflict between market value and fairness in the Marshallian sense of equal pay for work requiring equal natural ability and equally expensive training is brought out by the effect of the demand for science graduates. Should science teachers be paid more than teachers of history or languages who have followed a university course of equal length, equal expensiveness and have attained the same standard, because they can get more in industry? Should outside demand give the Professor of Engineering or Physics more than equally distinguished Professors of English or Classics?

In the case of four groups attempts have been made to find a way through these difficulties by devising more precise tests of comparability. The demand for the services of three—civil servants, doctors and dentists, and police—does not come from sales, but from monies provided by the State on the scale it determines, and there is not much movement of personnel between them and outside industry or callings. Their pay is thus in some degree insulated from market influences. On what basis shall it be determined? Railwaymen are paid partly out of sales revenue, but as demand is falling, they have been protected in some degree from the consequences to employment of attempts to keep rates comparable, by State aid. Technically comparisons are difficult. In clerical and administrative work the operations performed and output are not easily measurable, the precise duties and responsibilities of apparently similar grades vary and the great variety of 'wage for age' or incremental scales makes it necessary to determine whether to use an average or a median of the rates. Since police have a retiring age of 55, ought they not to have rates which provide in the shorter working life earnings comparable with occupations having a normal working life? The remarkable differences in the working life of the various professions is brought out in the Pilkington Commission on doctors' and dentists' remuneration.[1] How is one to translate into weekly pay the different values of pensions, gratuities, bonuses or to allow for awkward hours of duty?

The first breakthrough was made by the Priestley Commission on the *Civil Service*[2] (1955). Arguing that the basis should be fair comparison with the current remuneration of outside staffs on comparable work, it recommended the establishment of a fact-finding body (The Civil Service Pay Research Unit) to determine, in a selection of industries to be mutually agreed, what jobs were comparable and what pay and conditions attached to each. In the Unit's first annual report, it seemed to be the nature of the work rather than the qualifications asked for which make them comparable. The Pilkington Commission (Feb. 1960) made elaborate statistical comparisons of career earnings of doctors and dentists with those of other professions (e.g. architects, actuaries, solicitors, barristers, engineers) who had somewhat similar education and were recruited from a similar constituency. But it listed[3] a number of relevant factors (e.g. qualifications, length and cost of training, length of professional life, intellectual and other qualities) to be taken into account, although it is not apparent from the Report precisely how far they made use of or translated them into money terms in assessing

---

[1] *Doctors' and Dentists' Remuneration*. R. Com. Rep. See graphs pp. 3, 33, 35; 1959–60 Cmnd. 939, xii.

[2] *The Civil Service*. R. Com.; 1955–56 Cmd. 9613, xi. See P. and G. Ford, *Breviate of Parliamentary Papers, 1940–54;* pp. 38–9. *Civil Service Pay Research Unit*, First Ann. Rep. 1957, p. 9. 1958 Non-Parl. On the tests used, and the results, the reports are uninformative.

[3] Rep. para. 150.

the various professional scales, or merely looked at them in a more general way. Although it found that the doctor's median earnings were above, in one case double, those of other professions, it nevertheless decided that they were too low. In a dissenting report Professor Jewkes arrived at his own results more directly, but paid regard to a possible shortage of doctors, which the majority did not. The Guillebaud Committee on *Railway Pay*[1] (Mar. 1960) aided by a team of investigators, made a most thorough examination of the comparability of jobs and of the pay attached to them with those in other nationalized industries, public services and other private undertakings, using for the purpose a number of specific factors, such as the extent to which work was repetitive and involved initiative, supervision of others, degree of mental and nervous strain, etc. In this industry the demand for labour was falling, but in the police service there was a deficiency in the forces of some 14 per cent. The Willink Commission[2] (Nov. 1960) did not proceed straight from this to ask what rates of pay would encourage recruitment up to the required numbers, but rejected both 'supply and demand' (on the ground that police force pay should be insulated from market variations) and 'fair comparisons'. It did not undertake any detailed job-analysis to determine comparability of work, but taking as a basis the pay of 18 skilled crafts, added 40 per cent to make up for the lack of opportunities for extra earnings (overtime, etc.) and a further 25 per cent of the combined total to take account of a policeman's responsibilities in a disciplined service. This elaborate calculation is not as scientific as it looks, but it may well be that these guesses of 45 per cent and 25 per cent made by experienced people simply amounted to bringing the figures up to the total needed to secure the desired number of recruits of suitable quality. For in the long run a final test in this and other cases of awards is whether in the labour market they perform that function. Similarly, where industries are in decline or in economic difficulties, the application of a comparability rule irrespective of market conditions has some repercussion on employment.

[1] *Railway Pay.* Cttee. Rep. 1960. Published by the special Jt. Cttee. on Machinery of Negotiation for Railway Staff.
[2] *Police.* R. Com. Rep. pp. 53–9; 1960–61 Cmnd. 1222, xx. There is a good critical review of all four reports by H. A. Clegg, *Fair Wage Comparisons* in the *Journal of Industrial Economics*; 1960–61, pp. 199–314. See also, H. Smith, *The Wage Fixers.* 1962.

Next, there are claims based on the need to maintain and to restore the differentials for skill. What is a 'fair' differential? What is the 'proper' relationship between the skilled and unskilled man? The customary one? Professor Phelps Brown has shown that in the building trade the bricklayer's differential had, until World War I, been roughly unchanged for hundreds of years: that this could have been maintained for so long may, perhaps, have been due to a relatively static building technique and to a customary relationship between the number of skilled and the number of labourers. As Mr. Turner has shown, there was also a period of relative stability in differentials in engineering, though it is not so clear why these should not have been broken down more easily in an industry so exposed to change. Two world wars, the pressure of full employment in the market for unskilled labour and the practice of demanding flat rate increases which some unions with a dominantly unskilled or semi-skilled membership have adopted, has wrought some havoc with many customary differentials, so that what is now being demanded is both fair wages for comparable skill, and fair inequalities for unequal skill.

But what is 'comparable' skill? How much inequality is 'fair'? Is apprenticeship the test? On this ground the engineers said that their wages were too low compared with those of men in other industries who did not serve one—such as London postmen and bus drivers.[1] The craft unions in the iron and steel trades, who worked alongside production workers with earnings of £18 to £30 compared with their own £14, wanted to be lifted to a 'much higher wage band nearer that of the skilled operators on the process side'. But the employers argued that they were already getting more than their fellow craftsmen in the engineering industry. The unions representing production workers said with some acerbity that their men reached their highly skilled jobs not by an apprenticeship which terminated at twenty-one, but by an 'apprenticeship' of fifteen to twenty years working on the job before the requisite knowledge and experience were gained, and by working up through the ranks by promotion;[2] yet they complained that hundreds of craftsmen

[1] *Engineering and Allied Employers' National Federation and ... Confederation of Shipbuilding and Engineering Unions. Dispute.* Ct. of Inquiry. Rep. para. 27 (i); 1956–57 Cmnd. 159, xiv.

[2] *Iron and Steel Trades Employers' Association and the National Jt. Trade Unions' Craftsmen's Iron and Steel Cttee. Dispute.* Ct. of Inquiry. Rep. paras. 51, 67, 79; 1955–56 Cmd. 9843, xxi.

had left the iron and steel industry to take up work in other industries. How do we weigh the relative ability and time required for an apprenticeship training against the strain of driving a London bus? Or with the system of working up through grades of skill by promotion? Change of processes and the growth in old and new industries of jobs requiring varied degrees of knowledge and dexterity from unskilled, through semi-skilled to fully-skilled work has blurred many old distinctions. But we have fortunately not reached the stage of argumentation about fine differences which led an exasperated Australian wage court judge to exclaim: 'After all, it takes some skill to blow one's nose!'

Difficulties of another order begin in the claims of office white-collar workers. These also may want the 'old' differentials restored;[1] already working a shorter week than the manual operatives, they habitually follow the demand of the operatives for a shorter week with a claim for a shorter week still. When we move out of the clerical ranks within an industry to the higher scientific and professional level, whose commencing salary in the early years of earning may be not so much below the regular earnings of some operatives and whose maximum earnings far beyond them, both unions, courts and committees of inquiry have a new problem. T.U.C. is committed both to the principle of industrial unionism, which should theoretically include all workers until somewhere near the top 'owners' are excluded, and to defence of the right, certainly of those unions of better-paid grades affiliated to Congress and sometimes of unions not affiliated, to bargain as effectively for their members as they can. To decline to support them would not only shock the unions' conscience, but introduce an explosive element into Congress discussions. There is a difference between persuading a union to moderate its demands in order to secure a settlement of a conflict and asking it to accept a relative reduction of living standards. Congress now has to defend not only the under-dog, but dogs of more aristocratic breeds as well.

What influence have these claims of 'fairness' had on the whole process and results of bargaining? The most obvious fact is the

---

[1] For example, *Applications for an Improvement in Wages and Salaries made to the Railway Executive by the N.U.R., the A.S.L.E.F., and the Railway Clerks' Assoc.* Ct. of Inquiry. Rep. paras. 116–17; 1950–51 Cmd. 8154, xvi. Also, 500,000 white-collar workers' claim in the engineering industries for a 35-hour week. *The Times.* Jan. 16th, 1958. p. 10c.

relative rise in the wages of the unskilled, though this is not equally true over the whole field, nor is the degree of narrowing constant over time. Though the major cause of this is full employment, which has lifted unskilled labour out of its condition of chronic under employment, there are other reasons as well. As we have seen, a 'floor' has been put to wages, particularly agricultural wages, which have been raised partly for this reason, but most of all by the post-war policy of expanding agriculture and by the increase of mechanization, which has made some of the work comparable with, and call on, the same class of labour as industrial work. Then since World War I, and even since 1945, there has been an expansion of unionism amongst unspecialized and unskilled workers. The creation of great industrial unions and federations of all grades, which usually have a heavy weighting of the unskilled and less skilled members, makes for the same results. At the time of their formation it is not possible for the new union or federation to do other than accept the customary differentials, whatever they are. After its formation and when it is a going concern, it is very difficult for a union to discriminate between its grades of members when making a pay claim: all must in some sense be treated alike. Treating them alike may mean asking for the same flat rate increase or the same percentage increase, and many of these unions have, in fact, asked for the former, which narrows the differential in cash terms and in periods of rising prices, still more in real terms.

There are some limits to this process. First, as Mr. Turner[1] has shown, in unions in which the skilled worker is dominant, in which the admission to the upper grades is partly by promotion from the lower, and which in some cases have no membership outside their industry, e.g. miners, cotton-minders and some 'steel' unions, the differentials have not narrowed in this way, and have, indeed, sometimes widened. Secondly, the decline in the real value of any differential over a period of time may in due course set up strains between the skilled and the unskilled. This is clear where there is an outlet in the form of a rival union, as in the case of loco drivers. In some federations, where the craft unions retain their autonomy, there is possibly still some reserve power in their hands. Breakaway unions, on the other hand, are not easy to form in view of the

[1] H. A. Turner. 'Trade Unions, Differentials and the Levelling of Wages.' *Manchester School of Economic and Social Studies*, Vol. XX, 1952. p. 227. The article is an admirable analysis of the problem.

refusal of T.U.C. to recognize them, nor are transfers to other unions always easy in view of the Bridlington rules restricting them. Thirdly, where a union of a particular grade has members in more than one industry, different flat rate advances in the different industries may upset the ideal of a uniform rate for a particular skill or aptitude in whatever industry it works—the railway shopmen's problem. If one industry is expanding faster than another, it may be economically right for all grades to receive a rise in order to attract men, but a particular grade may rise in market value also because of an increased demand in some other industry, and failure to raise it, even at the expense of upsetting differentials, may result in an industry suffering from a shortage of that particular grade of labour. There is evidence that this occurs.

The effect on the differentials between manual and non-manual work is not completely clear. Some of the lower grades of clerical work are now less well paid than some of the grades of manual work, though this is not new nor is it surprising. For the change in the educational system, and the growth of the grammar schools have in some degree relieved the pressure of entrants into the manual grades, and increased it in the clerical grades, whose 'wage premium' has thus been removed or decreased; but J. S. Mill had pointed this out over a century ago.[1] On the other hand, the great growth of Government activities and of large industrial concerns, both nationalized and private, necessarily implies a growth in the demand for clerical work. Further, proper comparisons are made more difficult by the development of clerical pay scales with starting rates, annual increments and promotions from grade to grade, so that the final rate may be above, when the starting rate is below, that of many grades of manual workers. A number of circumstances may account for the fact that wages (often thought of as 'manual') increase faster than salaries over particular periods of time, and need not mean that the differentials are being narrowed

---

[1] J. S. Mill. *Principles of Political Economy.* Bk. II. Chap. IV. para. 2. 'Until lately, all employments which required even the humble education of reading and writing, could be recruited only from a select class, the majority having had no opportunity of acquiring these attainments. All such employments, accordingly, were immensely overpaid, as measured by the ordinary remuneration of labour. Since reading and writing have been brought within the reach of a multitude, the monopoly price of the lower grade of educated employments has greatly fallen, the competition for them having increased in an almost incredible degree. . . .'

correspondingly. But in all this we badly need a more exhaustive wages inquiry into the facts.

What effect have these characteristics of collective bargaining on the wage structure as a whole? First, as we saw on pp. 80, 81, it is possible for it to lead to a redistribution of the gains of collective bargaining as between workers in different industries. Next, the combined effect of full employment and bargaining by industrial unions and federations has been to bring about some redistribution of wages between the skilled and the unskilled. Thirdly, the combined effect of full employment, changing technology and developments in the educational system may have been to bring about some redistribution between the less well-paid clerical grades and some manual workers, though how much is not clear. These answers leave open the question of how far the awards and the forces generated by collective bargaining have really reshaped the basic wage structure, or how far they have simply provided a framework within which other economic and institutional influences, perhaps hindered and slowed down, continue to work.

(c) *Wage awards and the social hierarchy*

It has been argued that the awards of courts and the recommendations of committees accept and reflect, if they do not actually strengthen, the social values and social hierarchy of contemporary British society. The loco men asked that their 'proper value in relation to other railway grades' should be recognized, railway clerks and London compositors that their 'differentials' should be restored. Teachers should be able to enjoy a life of reasonably high cultural standards; the percentage of doctors with low incomes was too large and this profession should have a proper economic and social status; dentists' incomes should be thought of in relation to those of doctors. What are we to make of all this? Do these groups get their grade of pay 'because of' or 'to maintain' their 'social position'? Do those who recommend or determine the scales, most of them persons of good income and 'social position', just assume these social standards, thus making the social hierarchy self-perpetuating?

Two things already remarked upon have to be remembered. First, the arguments about the need to maintain conventional and social position have to be read as part of a statement of a case presented to the Court, into which the union will put whatever seems to strengthen it, and they should not be taken too readily at their face value. It is natural enough for a union to point out what desirable parts of its members' existing standard would be jeopardized if it did not get what it asked for, though sometimes the contentions are so naïve that the Court or Committee would be innocent indeed if it gave them more than a courtesy mention. Secondly, often union spokesmen are just trying to put into words a variety of considerations and personal preferences about the attractiveness or disadvantages of their occupation which in a non-unionized or competitive market would be gathered together and summed up by the movement of wage rates necessary to secure the number of workers demanded—the principle expressed by the Anderson Committee (p. 98).

The existence of non-competing layers of society with little vertical mobility between them has long been part of the stock-in-trade of economists, from Ricardo, who assumed long-term 'permanent' differences of wages, to Cairnes, Taussig and Cannan. The rigidity of the lines of division, the distance between them and the degree of upward movement vary with changing economic, educational and social circumstances. Cannan argued that since the cost of training for work in the better-paid grades could not be provided by all parents, the numbers entering them were limited, and therefore their wages and salaries were correspondingly higher. The labour market is 'layered' to receive entrants at the varying ages at which children leave the educational system: 15, 16, 18, 22 or 23, and so on. As the age rises, the numbers leaving and so competing for entry into occupations falls. It has been said that this can scarcely account for the existing differences of wage levels, since educational opportunities have been so greatly extended. But this overlooks the fact that much of that extension is recent, and that it will take time before the redistribution of the annual inflows of recruits to the various occupations exercises a marked competitive influence. And it also takes no account of the rightward shift of the demand curve. The expansion of the educational and social services, the demand for 'scientific manpower', the replacement of individual private enterprise by great trading organizations with large staffs and new methods of marketing and investigation, has enabled the economy to absorb entrants from the higher educational levels in far greater numbers than could have been envisaged before 1939. If this is the broad picture, the power of the Courts to make awards to maintain social and conventional position is restrained by the long-run operation of the market. There are plenty of people who would like to enjoy the incomes on which 'social position' is built, and competition for them would in the long run reduce any social position 'differential'. 'The economic mills may grind slowly, but they do grind.' If such differentials still exist, it is because restricted educational and other opportunities limit the numbers of those able to offer themselves for the better-paid occupations. It follows that those who wish to reduce the inequalities of earnings should look less to the manipulations of wages through the Courts than to more radical measures for removing institutional and educational limits on access to various kinds of work.

11. COLLECTIVE BARGAINING ALL ROUND WITH FULL EMPLOYMENT

What happens if unionization all round is combined with conditions of full employment? If there are more vacant jobs than men to fill them? We thus have rising wages in all trades, an increase of monetary demand and a tendency to inflation. A consequence is that relative wages seem to get out of gear. For some unions have more bargaining strength than others and are able to raise wages in their trade; an increased monetary demand means that more workers are needed in some trades, so that wages in them therefore rise. And full employment raises the relative demand for the large pool of unemployed labour which used to be fed by the unskilled or less skilled men, so that the pool disappears. Wage differentials therefore seem out of relation to what had been regarded as reasonable differences for skill, responsibility, etc., and unions make competitive demands to restore and correct them. This tendency is strengthened by 'wage drift', since individual employers, in an endeavour to retain staff or to cope with special conditions, can by various devices add substantially to the nationally agreed rate; and by competition these can spread. In these inflationary conditions wage increases do not 'come out of' and are not made at the expense of profits, for the employer can add the increase of his cost to his prices. When each industry secures an annual increase of money wages the cumulative effect may thus be both to make it more difficult for a union to secure and hold a rise in its position relatively to others[1] and to raise money incomes faster than

[1] See above, pp. 65, 106.

production. Its own rise of real wages is pared down by the increase of money wages obtained by others and this itself prompts further attempts to improve them. The self-frustrating nature of the rise in money incomes is shown by the fact that in fifteen years hourly earnings rose to two and a half times their 1946 figure, while real wages rose only by one-third.[1] The effect of the pursuit by individual unions of their own bargaining policies is thus 'to promote an end which was no part of their intention'.[2]

The problems thus pass out of the field of individual collective agreements into that of the cumulative effect of all of them, and open out wide questions of monetary, investment and fiscal policy which are outside the scope of this book. All one need say here is that for Britain it is necessary that export prices should not be out of relation with those of other countries, and that if we are to have fixed rates of exchange and full employment there is a limit to the increase of cost which can be accepted. We thus appear to be confronted by a choice either of continuing with bargaining by individual unions, ignoring its probable effect in leading eventually to a decline in the value of money, or of working out some new approach to or co-ordination of policy on the part of the unions. It is for this reason that unions have been urged to exercise 'wage restraint', to remember their 'social responsibilities', etc., and that official Government statements have been issued to explain why, under what conditions and to what extent such restraint would be desirable.[3] Such restraint implies, to a limited or greater extent, a co-ordinated or centralized wage policy on the part of the unions, and it might imply also that the Industrial Court, the Tribunal, Wages Councils and other wage-fixing bodies should adopt some point of view on the matter.

[1] E. H. Phelps Brown in *Industrial Relations, Contemporary Problems and Perspectives*, ed. B. C. Roberts, 1962, p. xiii. For all incomes see the graphical comparison of gross domestic incomes and gross domestic product at constant prices, for 1950–61. National Incomes Commission, *Scottish Plumbers' and Scottish Builders' Agreements of 1962*. p. 6; 1962–63 Cmnd. 1994.

[2] See speech of Birch. T.U.C., Bournemouth, Sept. 4th, 1958. Rep. pp. 417–18.

[3] *Price Stabilization and Industrial Policy*; 1940–41, Cmd. 6294, viii. *Personal Incomes, Costs and Prices*; 1947–48, Cmd. 7321, xxii. See also T.U.C., Margate, 1948. Report, p. 290. 'Trade Unions and the Economic Situation.' In, T.U.C., Margate, 1952, p. 285. 'T.U.C. and Wages Policy.' In, T.U.C., Brighton, 1950, p. 267.

There are two things to consider: what the theoretical objectives of such a co-ordinated policy should be and what its practical difficulties are. One major practical difficulty needs immediate mention because it colours the unions' whole approach to the problem, and that is their long and fiercely defended tradition that each union has the right to bargain with the employers without hindrance and to the best of its ability. So strong is it, indeed, that a foreign scholar has observed that in a world in which individual private enterprise has dwindled and both parties have embarked on measures of State intervention, British unions, despite their close connection with a Socialist political party, remain one of the last strongholds of individualism![1]

First, one possible objective would be to keep money wages constant, leaving increased productivity to show itself in falling prices. This has an additional merit in that, as we have seen earlier (pp. 69, 70), the gains of productivity are not retained in the form of higher money wages to workers in those industries which happen to be in a state of technical progress and where the unions are strong enough to secure a larger share of them, but are spread more evenly throughout the community. But it seems an impossible policy for a union to adopt, for it leaves them with no obvious function, especially as the traditional, friendly activities are taken over by the State; they would not set out to secure a rise, but just let prices fall. It would be difficult, indeed, to recruit and retain members on that basis.

Alternatively, the objective could be to let money wages rise with rising productivity, either according to the rise in average productivity in industry as a whole, or according to a rise in productivity in the individual industries. One preliminary misunderstanding should be removed. One trade union officer rejected any attempt to relate wages to productivity on the ground that it was impossible to measure the productivity, say, of a railway porter or railway clerk. But what is meant by productivity in this connection is not physical output, but the value of output, and that is measured daily when employers decide to add to or diminish their staffs. We can also leave aside the technical statistical difficulties of determining productivity, the fact that these indices take time to calculate

[1] See speech by Webber, Transport Salaried Staffs Association, T.U.C., Bournemouth, Sept. 4th, 1958. Congress rejected a proposal for a joint strike fund. pp. 436–7.

and are always a bit behind the times, and the rather different
question of deciding whether wage agreements should be based, not
on productivity in the immediate past, but what it is expected to be
during the future period of their currency. For whatever basis is
chosen for the index of 'average' productivity, the actual increase
of productivity in some industries will be greater and in others
smaller than the average; some industries will receive a smaller rise
of wages and others a larger rise than their own productivity
justifies. And if we assume that the industries in which productivity
is rising faster than the average are the ones which should be allowed
to draw in labour, pegging wages at the average increase will so far
diminish the incentive of workers to move into it. The policy might,
perhaps, be less difficult for the unions to operate than a policy of
constant money wages and falling prices, but it would not be
without snags of its own. For it would mean that miners' wages,
for example, were determined partly by the efforts and progress in
productivity of builders, railwaymen or engineers. The connection
between effort, productivity and wages would seem a little loose.

The second possibility would be to tie increases in wages in each
industry with the increases in productivity in that industry: wage
policy would not be centralized, but decentralized; the individual
unions would bargain as they do now, and push ahead wherever it
was possible on this basis.[1] There would be some squabbling over
what the exact rise of productivity was, and to whose fault any
lagging might be attributed, but these would be minor matters if
the principle were accepted. But fixing wages on this basis would
probably increase the wage differentials between industries, since
productivity would almost certainly increase faster in some industries than in others; and it would be very difficult to urge a union
in an advancing industry not to press for its full rise just to keep

[1] The Association of Supervisory Staffs, Executives and Technicians proposed to the National Joint Council for Civil Air Transport a three- or five-year
contract providing for an annual pay increase of 5 per cent or the percentage
increase in productivity, whichever was less. The Times. Mar. 17th, 1958.
p. 4e. Other long-term agreements include those by the printing unions in
1959, for three years, and by the building unions in 1963, which provide for
wage increases spread over three years and for considering the possibility of
relating wage changes to productivity instead of to retail prices. The Local
Government Officers 1963 Agreement provided for a rise of 3 per cent in each
of three years, the percentage obviously being based on the Government's
'guiding light'. The Times. Sept. 11th, 1963, 10c; Aug. 26th, 1963, 8c.

rates in the accustomed alignment. Some industries will grow, others lag, new industries will be established, and this requires a redistribution of labour, sometimes aided by a rise in wages in the expanding industries. When there are pools of unemployed men to draw from, such increases of wages need not be high, but in conditions of full employment they must be high enough to attract men from the jobs they are already in. The differentials needed to secure mobility may thus become large enough to seem 'unreasonable' to other trades, because they are related not to skill or unpleasantness of work, but to demand. As we have seen, the unions' attitude to differentials is not completely clear or settled. All we can say is that perhaps they do not want them to be 'too high'. But parity between growing and static industries there cannot be, if differences of wages are to be one means of redistributing labour.[1] If this mechanism is rejected or weakened, then either other means of directing labour have to be found, or we have to accept, as part of the order of things in the labour market, both a not fully efficient and rather creaky machinery for manning growing industries and a good deal of argumentation about fairness which will slow up its operation. In an economy such as ours, largely dependent on our capacity to adjust our production to the changes of the outside world, flexibility is important and it is well to keep these difficulties within moderate bounds.

But though the unions' bargaining policies cannot be fully considered outside their broader setting, they have in fact been given a distinct, if not separate place, in Government measures. From a theoretical point of view, a logical development of trade unionism all round and universal collective bargaining would be a single collective agreement covering the whole field. Or in a completely planned society a central body could as part of its planning decide first the total sum to be allocated to wages, salaries, etc., and by appropriate machinery divide that total amongst the separate industries and so on.[2] Interesting as it may be to play with the ideas these suggestions raise, they are scarcely practical issues. These are, in what ways we can avoid the recurrent exchange crises which have been a

---

[1] For a different view, see W. B. Reddaway, *Wage flexibility and the distribution of labour*, Lloyds Bank Review, Oct. 1959.

[2] As in Hungary. The increase was divided between new recruits to industry, and general increases, with special increases to those who had fallen behind. *The Times*, Dec. 27th, 1961, p. 11b.

consequence of internal inflation, and the damping down and loss of production which the measures taken to deal with them have brought about. That it is desirable to keep the long-term rate of increase in aggregate money incomes in step with the long-term rate of increase of national production is a widely accepted aim of policy. 'In step with', and not 'within' the rate of growth of production, because some have argued that the institutional pressures within the British economy make it unlikely in practice that we could do more than keep the inflationary rise of prices down to a moderate rate, say 3 per cent per annum.[1]

Two sources of inflation are recognized: an excess level of total demand, and an excessive rise in total money incomes. Government policy has tackled both. Sharp alterations of the bank rate, impositions and reductions of taxes, restrictions on and easing of hire purchase, and periodic endeavours to restrain Government spending have been used to curb excessive levels of demand. The result has been and indeed had to be, if the measures were to be effective, to introduce periodic 'stop and go' checks on the growth of production and so on the expansion of standards of living.

The other source of inflation is the increase of money incomes. Of these, the largest aggregate consists of incomes from wages and salaries, so that collective agreements come into review. There was thus a need and a search by the Government in successive steps for an incomes policy.

(1) In 1957 the Cohen Council of three independent persons was set up to survey prices, productivity and the level of incomes, 'having regard to the desirability of full employment and increasing the standards of life based on expanding production and reasonable stability of prices', in the hope that its reports would influence the opinion and policies of those concerned. The first report rejected a suggestion that there should be announced a maximum percentage by which wages should rise, in favour of a recommendation that for 1958 the increases should be below the average of recently preceding years, and that increases in industries whose productivity was rising fastest should not go up to the full extent of the rise of productivity, because sympathetic and inflationary increases in other industries would follow. But T.U.C. was hostile to any outside body, though

[1] For a comment on this see Council on Prices, Productivity and Incomes. 1st Rep., paras. 90–110, and conclusion, 17. 1958, Non-Parl.

124   THE ECONOMICS OF COLLECTIVE BARGAINING

armed with means of making a detailed survey of the facts, being
empowered to prescribe the limits of unions' wage policies; in any
case the influence of its views on trade union opinion could be
rendered nugatory by the resistance of left-wing unions.

(2) During an emergency in July 1961 a temporary wage pause
was imposed on wages and salaries within the sector of public
employment—on civil service and national health service employees
—and on other workers awards for which the Minister's approval
was required.

(3) In February 1962 a Government White Paper on *Incomes
Policy: the Next Step*,[1] besides announcing the end of the wage pause,
in effect transferred the responsibility for providing 'a guiding light'
from the Cohen Council to the Government, on the ground that this
might be more authoritative and acceptable. Following a line
which the Cohen Council had earlier rejected, it said that for
1962 increases of wages and salaries (including cost of living adjustments) and other incomes should not exceed 2 per cent to $2\frac{1}{2}$ per
cent. In pursuit of this it asked that all wage negotiations be conducted with this figure in mind, and that less weight than heretofore
should be given to questions of comparability and to the trend of
profitability in particular industries. Independent arbitrators, who
habitually considered the cases before them only as between the
parties, should also be aware of the wider implications of their
awards. In fact, the arbitrators found this impracticable or for
various reasons did not follow the guidance, awards to civil servants, almoners and others reaching 4 per cent, 8 per cent, and even
13 per cent.

(4) Following the line of thought that wage settlements and wage
awards made independently of one another could, in full employment, have cumulative effects on the economy as a whole, in
November 1962 a small, independent National Incomes Commission
was established. This was to inquire into and make recommendations on any wage claim referred to it by the parties concerned,
or by a Minister where the cost was met wholly or partly from the
Exchequer or where he wished their view on any particular settlement other than an arbitration award. They were to have regard
not only to the circumstances of the case, but particularly to the
repercussions of the award on the economy as a whole, i.e. to the

[1] *Incomes Policy: the Next Step*; 1961–62. Cmnd. 1626.

THE THEORY OF COLLECTIVE BARGAINING

'National Interest' which became, as it were, a third party in the case. The first wage agreement referred to it indicates the purpose of the policy. A section (5,000 to 6,000) but not all of Scottish plumbers, engaged in jobbing work secured an agreement reducing the normal working week from forty-two to forty hours without loss of pay, so that the standard rate per hour was increased above that of other Scottish plumbers and was higher than that of other building operatives and for a shorter week. In the interests of parity this was followed by a similar agreement for 80,000 Scottish building trade operatives, who then had higher pay than the 800,000 building trade operatives in England and Wales. After a detailed investigation the Commission regarded both agreements as unjustified and contrary to the national interest.[1]

All these experiments in incomes policy have been treated with hostility by T.U.C., which has declined co-operation with any of them.[2] It objected to outside bodies being empowered to investigate or comment on negotiated wage agreements or to prescribe a general wage policy which unions should follow, to a wage pause limited to sections of workers in Government employment or whose wages were subject to Ministerial approval. It could scarcely be expected to accept wage restraint unless there were also limits to profits and other incomes, on which it did not accept Government assurances. Even these features of the policy might have looked a little less objectionable had it been formulated in the background of an expansion of the economy. For T.U.C. had criticized the other part of Government policy, that of restraining excess demand in ways which, it argued, damped down investment and production when they should have been expanding.

(5) The Government stated that the policy set out in the White Paper was an interim one only, designed to replace the wages pause until a more long-term one could be framed on the basis of co-ordinated plans for expansion and production targets for the main sectors of the economy. The reactions of employers and

[1] National Incomes Commission, *Scottish Plumbers' and Scottish Builders' Agreements of 1962*, paras. 110, 196; 1962–63. Cmnd. 1994.
[2] The annual reports of the T.U.C. from 1958 contain the text of statements and criticisms of Government policy, including the crisis measures of 1957. The report for 1962 and the debates on it, give a full statement of the views on the pay pause, National Incomes Commission and the National Economic Development Council. See especially Woodcock's speech, pp. 366–70.

unions to the wages pause and the Incomes Commission had made it clear that their co-operation was fundamental to success. After some preliminary sparring about the constitution, T.U.C. decided (1962) to be represented on and to participate in the work of a National Economic Development Council, provided that it could participate as a side, that no subject (such as profits and dividends) was excluded from discussion, and that it was not committed in any way. The Council was to have its own independent expert staff. Its objects were to examine plans in the public and private sectors, to consider the obstacles to quicker growth and if possible to secure agreement on the ways of accelerating it. The first task it undertook was to study the implications for the main components of the economy—manpower, investment, and the balance of payments— of an average growth of production of 4 per cent for the period 1961–66, a total of 22 per cent. From the thorough and balanced survey of inter-related quantities we pick out one item for note only because of its relevance to the narrower question with which these varied experiments in policy had been concerned. The target growth implied a 2·8 per cent annual increase of consumption per head in real terms, as compared with an increase of output of 3·3 per cent per head, the balance being savings.[1] To keep the price level stable, the rise in money incomes would have to be less rapid than the past average of 5–6 per cent a year.[2]

The unions have thus to reach some critical decisions on how to deal with the consequences on other unions of the jealously guarded traditional right of each union to do the best for its members in its own labour market, without reference to the effects on others. Are they, as in the experiments in Sweden and the Netherlands,[3] to try as a united body to agree each year with the employers or the employers and the Government, what the broad percentage rise of earnings should be and place on the individual industries the task of sorting out their own agreements so that they are in line with the general policy or, committed for

[1] *Growth of the United Kingdom Economy to 1966.* National Economic Development Council, p. vii, 17.

[2] *Conditions of Faster Economic Growth*, p. 51. National Economic Development Council.

[3] B. C. Roberts. *National Wages Policy in War and Peace*, 1958. Chaps. 6, 8. *Sweden: Its Unions and Industrial Relations.* T.U.C., 1963. T. L. Johnston, *Collective Bargaining in Sweden*, 1962. For recent Netherlands experience, see *The Times*. Sept. 29th, 1963.

years to economic planning as a policy, can they support planning over the whole field for everything except so important a component as wages and salaries? While unions' opinions are crystallizing one may expect shifts in the support for alternative courses, such as the rejection of wage restraint or acceptance of it on condition of the control of profits or of participation in the planning of expansion. The debates of the T.U.C. at Brighton 1963 showed a marked movement of opinion, rather more in speeches than in somewhat inconsistent voting.[1] Starting from the principle that planning in a free society must be based on the voluntary co-operation of those concerned in preparing and carrying out the plan, the General Council's report on *Economic Development and Planning*, which received overwhelming support, envisaged that these required common working between unions as bargaining and participating units, considerable changes in their organization, and in some degree common policy on wages. The need for a tidier and more effective allocation of the field between the unions, for a consideration of the place of workshop bargaining and representation, for larger and more uniform contributions from members, already called for by the conditions of industry-wide bargaining conditions of full employment, would be greatly increased. But further questions are suggested either by the Council in its report or by foreign experience. How could the gains of local bargaining over and above national rates with their bonuses, piece rates, etc., be kept in line with national agreements so as to limit the contribution of wage-drift to inflation? Technical changes mean that some industries expand, some contract: is redundancy to be met by more flexibility as an alternative to emphasis on job-security? Would the central body have to be given much more authority to speak for and perhaps commit the unions than heretofore? To prevent the plan from being jeopardized, would it be necessary for collective agreements to be made legally enforceable during the period of their operation, as in some countries, and for strikes during the period of the agreement, and unofficial strikes anyway, to be prohibited or

[1] See Speeches by Woodcock, Allen, Green, Douglass, Chapple, Dutton, Carron. T.U.C., Brighton, Sept. 4th, 1963. A motion opposing wage restraint in any form was carried by under 400,000 votes in a total of 8 million. The resolution that wage restraint was unacceptable without control of incomes from profits and capital gains was only formally expressing unions' repeated declarations.

K

penalized? Or could it be assumed that in an atmosphere of planned expansion these would become infrequent? Would this deal adequately with the problem of rebellious shop stewards? Would not this all mean that unions would require more officers, more intensively trained ones? The problems of policy thus have consequences reaching right down through union organization. Experience has been gained and progress made; but no democratic country with free trade unions has yet been able to produce a full solution of these problems, which call not only for vision, but for intense and persistent intellectual effort.

BIBLIOGRAPHY

THE literature on the economic aspects of trade unionism is extensive. The annual reports of Trades Union Congress are essential. Full references for the numerous disputes, wage inquiries and awards discussed have been given in footnotes to the text. But as this book is concerned with examining these in the light of recent and contemporary economic theory on collective bargaining, the following short list gives a number of other books and articles in which expositions or criticisms of the theory stated or implied in the argument can be found.

1. On labour's weakness in bargaining.

Marshall, A.	*Principles of Economics.* 8th ed. 1930. Bk. VI, chaps. III–V.
Marshall, A.	*Economics of Industry.* 3rd ed. 1889. Bk. VI, chap. IV.
Hutt, W. H.	*The Theory of Collective Bargaining.* 1930. A critical review of the accepted doctrines.

2. Trade Unions and Wages and Employment.

Marshall, A., and Marshall, M. P.	*The Economics of Industry.* 1879. Bk. III, chaps. VI, VII.
Thompson, H. M.	*The Theory of Wages and its Application to the Eight Hours Question and other Labour Problems.* 1902. pp. 115–24.
Marshall, A.	*Principles of Economics.* 8th ed. 1930. pp. 381–7, 698–710.
Marshall, A.	*Economics of Industry.* 3rd ed. 1889. Bk. VI, chap. XIII.
Macgregor, D. H.	*Industrial Combinations.* 1906. Reprinted 1935. Pt. II, chap. III.
Hoxie, R. F.	*Trade Unionism in the United States.* 1919.
Hamilton, W. H., and May, S.	*The Control of Wages.* 1923.
Hamilton, W. H.	'A Theory of the Rate of Wages.' *The Quarterly Journal of Economics*, August. 1922.
Dobb, M. H.	*Wages.* 1928. Chaps. V, VII.

Dobb, M. H.	'A Sceptical View of the Theory of Wages.' *Economic Journal*, XXXIX. 1929. p. 506.
Rowe, J. W. F.	*Wages in Practice and Theory.* 1928.
Shove, G. F.	Review of Hicks' *Theory of Wages*, in *Economic Journal*, September 1933. esp. pp. 470–2.
Robinson, J.	*The Economics of Imperfect Competition.* 1933. Chaps. 23–26.
Ross, A. M.	*Trade Union Wage Policy.* 1948.
Dunlop, J. T.	*Wage Determination under Trade Unions.* 1950. esp. chap. V.
Wootton, B.	*The Social Foundations of Wage Policy.* 1955.
Dunlop, J. T. (ed.)	*The Theory of Wage Determination.* 1957.
Brown, E. H. P.	*The Growth of British Industrial Relations.* 1959.
Robertson, D. J.	*Factory Wage Structures and National Agreements.* 1960.
Lerner, S., and Marquand, J.	'Workshop Bargaining, Wage Drift . . .' *Manchester School.* xxx, 1962.

3. Trade Unions in more than one trade.

Zeuthen, F.	*Problems of Monopoly and Economic Warfare.* 1930. pp. 124–7.

4. Bilateral Bargaining and Economic Warfare.

Pigou, A. C.	*Principles and Methods of Industrial Peace.* 1905.
Pigou, A. C.	*The Economics of Welfare.* 1921. Pt. III, chap. VI.
Zeuthen, F.	*Problems of Monopoly and Economic Warfare.* 1930. Chap. IV.
Hutt, W. H.	*The Theory of Collective Bargaining.* 1930. pp. 48–108.
Dunlop, J. T. (ed.)	*The Theory of Wage Determination.* 1957. Pt. V, chaps. 18, 19.

5. Fair Wages, Unfair Wages and Exploitation.

Pigou, A. C.	*The Economics of Welfare.* 1921. Pt. III, chaps. XI–XVI.
Pigou, A. C.	*The Economics of Welfare.* 4th ed. reprinted 1946. Pt. III, chaps. XII–XVII.
Shove, G. F.	Review of Hicks' *Theory of Wages*, in *Economic Journal*, September 1933. pp. 466–9.

6. Arbitration and Conciliation.

Pigou, A. C.	*Principles and Methods of Industrial Peace.* 1905.
Pigou, A. C.	*The Economics of Welfare.* 1921. Pt. III, chaps. I–VI.
Pigou, A. C.	*The Economics of Welfare.* 4th ed. reprinted 1946. Pt. III, chaps. I–VI.
Clay, H.	*The Problem of Industrial Relations.* 1929. Chap. VIII. esp. pp. 179–80.
Rankin, M. T.	*Arbitration Principles and the Industrial Court. An Analysis of Decisions, 1919–1929.* 1931.
Turner, H. A.	*Arbitration: a Study of Industrial Experience.* (Fabian Research Series No. 153) [1952].
Smith, H.	*The Wage Fixers.* 1962.

7. Trade Unions in Full Employment

Soule, G.	'The Relation between Wages and National Production.' *Annals of the American Academy of Political and Social Sciences*, March 1922.
Turvey, R. (ed. and transl.)	*Wages Policy under Full Employment.* 1952. Essays by four Swedish economists, E. Lundberg, R. Meidner, G. Rehn and K. Wickman.
Jack, D. T.	'Is a Wages Policy Desirable or Practicable?' *Economic Journal*, December 1957. p. 585.
Roberts, B. C.	*National Wages Policy in War and Peace.* 1958.
Johnston, T. L.	*Collective Bargaining in Sweden.* 1962.

8. Strikes

Knowles, K. G. J. C.	*Strikes: A Study in Industrial Conflict.* 1952.

9. Government and Organization of Trade Unions

Allen, V. L.	*Power in Trade Unions.* 1954.
Roberts, B. C.	*Trade Union Government and Administration in Great Britain.* 1956.
Allen, V. L.	*Trade Union Leadership.* 1957.

Industrial Relations Handbook; 1961 Non-Parl. Min. of Labour.

10. Industrial Relations in General.

For the Parliamentary Papers on this topic see relevant sections of:
Select List of British Parliamentary Papers, 1833–1899.
A Breviate of Parliamentary Papers, 1900–1916.
A Breviate of Parliamentary Papers, 1917–1939.
A Breviate of Parliamentary Papers, 1940–1954.

INDEX

EACH trade union is listed under the operative word in its title as given in the Annual Report of the Trades Union Congress: e.g. Railwaymen, National Union of